HARNESSING LEADERSHIP, IDEAS, PEOPLE AND STRATEGY

The 'LIPS' Framework for Business

Peter Sinodinos

First published in Australia by Aurora House
www.aurorahouse.com.au

This edition published 2024
Copyright © Peter Sinodinos 2024

Cover design: Donika Mishineva (www.artofdonika.com)
Typesetting and e-book design: Amit Dey (amitdey2528@gmail.com)

 A catalogue record for this book is available from the National Library of Australia

The right of Peter Sinodinos to be identified as Author of the Work has been asserted in accordance with the Copyright,
Designs and Patents Act 1988.

ISBN number: 978-1-923298-07-1 (paperback)

All rights reserved. No part of this publication may be reproduced, stored in a retrieval system, or transmitted, in any form or by any means without the prior written permission of the publisher, nor be otherwise circulated in any form of binding or cover other than that in which it is published and without a similar condition being imposed on the subsequent purchaser.

Distributed by: Ingram Content: www.ingramcontent.com
Australia: phone +613 9765 4800 | email lsiaustralia@ingramcontent.com
Milton Keynes UK: phone +44 (0)845 121 4567 | email enquiries@ingramcontent.com
La Vergne, TN USA: phone +1 800 509 4156 | email inquiry@lightningsource.com

DEDICATION

To my father Dennis and my mother California, who made it their mission to give my siblings, Arthur and Kathleen, and me the best start in life, sacrificing all they had to make it a reality. We are forever indebted to you. And to my wife Sharon, who has always believed in me and encouraged me to follow my dreams.

ACKNOWLEDGEMENTS

There are many people I'd like to acknowledge, but as space is limited, I will call out only a select few who have had the most profound effect on me to date. As for the rest – you know who you are!

Firstly, I'd like to express my deepest gratitude to Michael Headberry of Retail Synergy. As a pseudo mentor, his guidance and patience as we travelled across Europe and the Northern Hemisphere on study tours visiting iconic retailers such as Best Buy and Future Shop in the US; Boulanger and Darty in France; and Dixons, Currys, Asda, Comet and Marks & Spencer in the UK opened my eyes to the world of international retail. His assistance in helping me develop my understanding of deeper retail concepts and the metrics that matter has been invaluable.

A heartfelt thank you also goes to Andrew Muir and his father, the late Ian Muir – forever Essendon supporters – for the incredible opportunities they provided me through The Good Guys retail business here in Australia. Their trust allowed me to grow from a Business Development Manager to Group General Manager of Retail Operations and helped shape my career in property management, procurement and executive business management. I am also grateful to Michael Ford, CEO of The Good Guys at the time, for showing me the complexities of management styles and how to navigate challenging landscapes. Their insights were instrumental in my professional development and gave me perspective in terms of human nature.

My appreciation also goes to the late Geoff Brash, former chairman of Brash Electrical, and his family. Geoff's investment and training helped to ignite and fast-track my career in retail, along with the careers of many others.

Finally, a special thank you to my wife Sharon who has been my rock, picking me up from my lowest points and celebrating with me during the highest; my children for their love and understanding; and my siblings Arthur and Kathleen for their unwavering support and encouragement over the years.

I would not be where I am today without all these wonderful people.

CONTENTS

Foreword	xiii
A Note from the Author	xv
1. Introducing the LIPS Framework	1
2. Leadership	5
Leadership and vision	5
Great leadership – the catalyst for change	10
Leadership styles and their impact	11
Who are the stakeholders in leadership?	14
Eight ways to build gravitas	15
Six leadership tests/refreshers	16
Good role models	30
Leading with a passion for people's success	31
Leading like a rhino	33
Ten qualities of a great leader	35
What is extreme leadership?	36
Five signs of courage in leadership	37
The GARY Principle	38
The management skills matrix	40

The concept of VUCA	40
From VUCA to VUCAAC	41
Creativity in leadership	42
Daily principles to live by	45
The interplay of business strategy, leadership and people	45
A summary of leadership	47
3. Ideas	**51**
Five tried-and-tested exercises	52
Ideas = the seeds of innovation	53
Developing the seeds	54
Implementing ideas into action	55
Changing management in the ideation realm	56
The role of technology	57
A summary of ideas strategy	58
Inspirational ideas people	60
4. People	**65**
The critical role of people in organisations	65
Coaching for effective leadership	68
Helping people find their true purpose	68
Developing success from failure	69
Resolving work-related anxiety	71
Visual thinking methodology	73
Team dynamics: forming–storming–norming–performing	75
The Head, Heart and Hands Approach	78
The Iceberg Principle	79
Applying the Head, Heart and Hands philosophy	80

The Johari Window	85
Deliver the 5 to Survive!	87
Transforming your team dynamics	88
The Change Management Curve	89
8-to-be-great Maslow's pointers	91
Conflict coaching	91
Becoming a Coaching Warrior	93
People projects	95
Finding the right mentor	96
Seven tips for high-performance coaching	97
Seven tips for one-on-one coaching	98
Technology and people: the top 10 impacts in the sales world	98
Changing methodologies and diversity	103
Incentive programs for multi-generational teams	104
Coaching multi-generational personalities	106
The psychology of winning	112
The '3 Cs' of talent management and the '7 Cs' of communication	114
Change x 3	115
Effective communication and presentation skills	116
Smart and fast goal setting	117
The power of great storytelling	118
The 9-box Leadership and Matrix	119
Job description on a page	119
Acronyms to remember	121

5. Strategy — 123

Understanding the components of strategic planning	127
Leadership steps in strategy alignment	128
Adaptive strategies in business	129
Leadership and strategic execution	130
Key aspects of strategic execution	132
Strategy and innovation	134
The P.E.S.T.L.E.D. analysis method	136
SWOT: Looking for the gaps	137
Volume mix and rate: The VMR index	138
Business lifecycles	138
The D.E.C.K.S. hypothesis	139
SPAMBOTS: My top eight strategies for success	140
Acquisition, Conversion and Retention (ACR)	142
The 100-day plan	144
Continuous problem solving	144
Kaizen power	145
The art of selling	146
Value disciplines	147
Strive for 5	148
Eight steps for setting up benchmarking	149
The 9 vital vanilla strategies	150
Procrastination and the PNR strategy	151
Mintzberg's '5 Ps of Strategy'	152
The Diamond Model	153
Case Study: The McDonald's model	156

Useful micro strategies to try	158
Seven micro strategies for defending the core	159
Bowman's strategy	160
Blue Ocean strategy	163
The 5Ps: a tried and tested comprehensive marketing framework	165
The Retail Pentagon	166
Strategy and culture: partners in business performance	168
The value of a Venn diagram	169
Porter's Five Forces	169
Conclusion	**171**
Bibliography	**175**
About the Author	**179**

FOREWORD

by Arthur Sinodinos

When I look back on the career my younger brother, Peter, has carved out for himself over the past three decades, I feel a deep sense of pride. As someone who has walked the corridors of politics, served as an ambassador, and navigated the complex world of business, I've seen my fair share of leaders, leadership and strategy. Yet, Peter's approach to these principles is fresh, thought provoking and imminently practical.

From his early days in retail, Peter demonstrated an extraordinary ability to bring out the best in the people around him. He understands that leadership is not only about giving orders or setting a direction; it is about connecting with people, understanding their needs, and leading with empathy. This is a quality I have always admired in him, not just as a brother, but as someone who innately grasps the importance of empathy in leadership across different sectors.

Peter is always passionate about ideas, constantly seeking out new ways to innovate and improve, never settling for the status quo. He has an uncanny ability to recognise a good idea when he sees it and the determination to see it through, no matter the obstacles. His commitment to staying a student of strategy, always learning, refining and adapting, has been a cornerstone of his education and business success. These principles, Leadership, Ideas, People and Strategy, are the foundation of what Peter calls the LIPS framework. It's a framework that has not only guided his career but has also influenced many of the businesses and teams he has worked with over the years. I've had the privilege of witnessing the hard work Peter has put into this framework firsthand, seeing how it transforms organisations and empowers individuals to achieve their best.

In this book, Peter shares the wisdom and insights he has gained from over thirty years in the retail industry, distilled into the LIPS framework. Whether you're a business leader, an entrepreneur, or someone looking to make a difference in your career, I believe you will find great value in Peter's approach. It's a testament to his dedication, his passion for helping others succeed, and his relentless pursuit of personal excellence.

As his older brother, I've always known that Peter was destined for great things. This book reflects that journey, and I'm honoured to write this foreword. I hope you find it inspiring and practical as you navigate the complexities of modern business life.

~ Hon. Arthur Sinodinos AO

A NOTE FROM THE AUTHOR

As a professional executive with over thirty-five years of business leadership experience, the subject of a business's greatest asset – its people – has always been close to my heart. While some choose to treat people as human capital, I have always been fascinated by the way we can work with our employees to get the best performance from them through self-discovery and coaching.

A few months ago, while attending the 80th birthday celebration of an old mentor, we got talking about this very subject. During our conversation, we found ourselves delving into the significance of people in business. Our discussion spanned topics such as understanding strategy formation, leveraging new ideas for innovation and growth, and demonstrating strong, positive leadership to drive results and transformative change. As my mentor reminded me, perseverance is 90% of the leadership equation, where applying your knowledge and experience in people to mentor and coach them gets the best results. The balance – the remaining 10% – can be allocated to your own creativity and to add 'spice' to your leadership style.

Inspired by this exchange and buoyed by many years of encouragement from other colleagues in the business world, I found myself embarking on a daily blogging challenge on my LinkedIn profile, exploring these interconnected themes. My blogs received such positive feedback that I was motivated to produce this book – a collection of adapted blogs that explore the concepts of Leadership, Ideas, People and Strategy – or 'LIPS' for short. Manage the LIPS concepts well, or create a business environment where they thrive, and you will have success.

Thank you for taking the time to read my book. I hope you find it insightful and engaging. I would love to connect with you on LinkedIn to continue the conversation and share more ideas. You can find me at: https://petersinodinos.com

I look forward to hearing from you!

~ Peter Sinodinos

1. INTRODUCING THE LIPS FRAMEWORK

The LIPS framework represents the essential elements that drive organisational success:

- **Leadership** sets the tone, guiding the ship through turbulent waters;
- **Ideas** fuel innovation, sparking creativity and growth;
- **People** form the heart of any enterprise, their collective efforts shaping its destiny; and finally
- **Strategy** provides the roadmap, aligning actions with purpose.

Together, these interconnected facets create a harmonious symphony, orchestrating achievement and transformation within an organisation, akin to the interwoven strands of DNA within a living creature. Business strategy sets the direction for the organisational journey, while leadership strategy acts as the human enabler, breathing life into the business plan.

Effective leaders understand that their role extends beyond mere execution; they must foster interpersonal dynamics, prioritise well-being and enhance job satisfaction among team members. By integrating these strategies, organisations can unlock their full potential and navigate the complexities of today's uncertain environment.

Let's first look at the inter-relationships between the four essential components of LIPS.

L. What role does *Leadership* play?

- Leadership involves guiding and inspiring the organisation towards its goals.
- Effective leaders set the vision, create a conducive culture to allow this vision to eventuate and make strategic decisions.

So, what is leadership's inter-relationship with ideas, people and strategy?

- **Ideas:** Leaders often foster a culture of innovation by encouraging the generation and implementation of new ideas. They must be open to diverse thinking and perspectives to harness the creative potential within the organisation.
- **People:** Leaders are responsible for building and nurturing talent. They must understand the strengths and weaknesses of their team members, providing support and motivation to maximise their potential.
- **Strategy:** Leaders are the architects of strategy. They must align the organisation's vision with actionable plans, ensuring that resources are allocated efficiently and goals are achievable.

I. What role do *Ideas* play?

- Ideas represent the innovative and creative solutions that propel a business forward.
- They are the foundation for new products, services and processes that can provide a competitive edge.

So, how do ideas interact with and entwine themselves in leadership, people and strategy?

- **Leadership:** Innovative ideas often need the support and endorsement of leaders to be implemented. Leaders play a crucial role in creating an environment where ideas can flourish and be tested.

- **People:** Ideas typically originate from people within the organisation. A diverse and inclusive workforce can bring a wide range of perspectives and experiences, leading to richer and more innovative ideas.
- **Strategy:** Ideas need to be aligned with the overall strategy of the organisation. Strategic planning ensures that the best ideas are pursued and integrated into the broader goals of the business.

P. **What role do *People* play?**

- People are the human capital of the organisation, providing the skills, knowledge and effort necessary to achieve business objectives.
- They are the source of innovation, productivity and organisational culture.

So, how do people inter-relate with leadership, ideas and strategy?

- **Leadership:** Effective leadership is crucial in managing and developing people. Leaders must inspire, mentor and support their teams to drive engagement and performance.
- **Ideas:** People are the originators and implementers of ideas. A motivated and skilled workforce is more likely to generate valuable ideas and successfully bring them to fruition.
- **Strategy:** People execute the strategic plans set by leadership. Ensuring that the right people are in the right roles is essential for effective strategy implementation.

S. **What role does *Strategy* play?**

- Strategy defines the long-term direction and actions that a business will take to achieve its goals.
- It involves setting objectives, analysing the competitive environment and allocating resources.

So, how does strategy inter-relate with leadership, people and ideas?

- **Leadership:** Leaders are responsible for formulating and communicating the strategy. They must ensure that the strategy is clear, realistic and adaptable to changing conditions.
- **Ideas:** Strategic planning should incorporate innovative ideas to stay competitive. A good strategy leverages new ideas to create value and differentiate the business in the market.
- **People:** Successful strategy execution depends on the people within the organisation. Their skills, dedication and teamwork are critical to achieving strategic objectives.

Now that we have a broad understanding of the inter-relationship between leadership, ideas, people and strategy as being fundamental in modern-day business, to recap: remember that *Leadership* sets the tone and direction, *Ideas* drive innovation and progress, *People* are the executors and enablers of those ideas, and *Strategy* provides the roadmap for achieving organisational goals. When these elements are aligned and work together harmoniously, businesses are better positioned to thrive in a competitive and ever-changing environment.

In the following chapters, we will break down each of the elements of the framework to get a deeper understanding of their importance to each other.

2. LEADERSHIP

Leadership is the ability to influence and guide individuals or groups towards the achievement of goals. Effective leadership is paramount in any organisation as it sets the tone, builds the culture and drives the vision forward. Leaders inspire, motivate and provide direction, ensuring that all members of the organisation are aligned and working towards a common purpose.

Leadership and vision
A compelling vision is a fundamental aspect of effective leadership. It provides a sense of direction and purpose, aligning the organisation's efforts towards a common goal. Visionary leaders can articulate a clear and inspiring vision that resonates with employees and stakeholders alike. Let's call this a 'compelling vision'.

There are four components of a compelling vision:

1. **Clear**

    The vision should be clear and understandable, providing a straightforward path to follow.

2. **Inspirational**

    The vision should motivate and inspire employees to go above and beyond their normal duties.

3. **Challenging**

   A good vision sets ambitious, yet achievable, goals that push the organisation towards excellence.

4. **Future-oriented**

   A compelling vision focuses on long-term goals and the desired future state of the organisation.

Leadership also plays an important role in vision implementation. Leaders must communicate this vision effectively, ensuring that all employees understand and are committed to it. This is the best way to ensure that organisational strategies, goals and actions are aligned with their vision and allows them to provide the necessary resources, training and support to help employees achieve it. A transparent approach and the ability to be adaptable allows leaders to be open to refining the vision as circumstances change, ensuring it remains relevant and attainable.

Effective leadership requires a diverse set of competencies and skills. Some of the key competencies include:

1. **Emotional intelligence.** This is the ability to understand and manage one's own emotions and those of others. A high level of emotional intelligence enables leaders to build strong relationships, resolve conflicts and create a positive work environment.

2. **Communication.** Effective communication is crucial for conveying vision, goals and expectations. It involves active listening, clear articulation and the ability to persuade and inspire.

3. **Decision making.** Leaders must be able to make informed decisions quickly, often under pressure. This requires analytical thinking, problem-solving skills and the ability to weigh various options and outcomes.

4. **Adaptability.** The business environment is constantly changing, and leaders must be flexible and adaptable to navigate new challenges and opportunities.

5. **Strategic thinking.** The ability to think long term, anticipate future trends and plan accordingly is essential Strategic thinkers can align short-term actions with long-term goals.
6. **Integrity.** Trustworthiness and ethical behaviour are foundational to effective leadership. Leaders with integrity inspire confidence and respect from their team members.

These skills may come naturally to some, while other leaders will develop them as they grow as part of an orchestrated leadership development program for their organisation or board.

Investing in leadership development is essential for creating a pipeline of capable leaders who can drive the organisation's success. Effective leadership development programs focus on building the competencies and skills necessary for current and future leadership roles.

The best way to develop these skills is through core Leadership Development Programs (LDP). Components of these programs include:

- Training and workshops that cover various aspects of leadership, including communication, emotional intelligence, strategic thinking and decision making.
- Active mentorship and leadership coaching where new leaders are paired up with experienced mentors who can provide guidance, support and feedback.
- Experiential Learning (EL), where opportunities for leaders to gain hands-on experience through projects, assignments and real-world challenges are allocated by CEOs, board members or mentors.
- A consistent assessment and feedback program to identify strengths and areas for improvement, coupled with constructive feedback to support development.
- Lastly – and the most critical – succession planning to identify and prepare potential leaders to fill key roles in the organisation's future.

Effective leadership is not without its challenges. Some of the most common challenges leaders face include:

- **Managing change**

  Leading an organisation through change can be difficult, as it often involves overcoming resistance and maintaining morale.

- **Balancing multiple priorities**

  Leaders must juggle various responsibilities and priorities, ensuring that all aspects of the organisation are aligned and functioning effectively.

- **Navigating uncertainty**

  In today's rapidly changing business environment, leaders must be able to navigate uncertainty and make decisions with incomplete information.

- **Building and maintaining trust**

  Trust is a critical component of effective leadership. Leaders must consistently demonstrate integrity and reliability to build and maintain trust with their team members.

- **Developing future leaders**

  Ensuring that there is a continuous pipeline of capable leaders requires ongoing effort and investment in leadership development.

So, what does all this mean for the future of leadership?

As the business environment continues to evolve, so too must leadership practices. The future of leadership will likely be characterised by increased emphasis on emotional intelligence. As organisations recognise the importance of emotional intelligence in building strong relationships and fostering a positive work culture, leaders with high emotional intelligence will be in high demand.

The same can be said of having a greater focus on diversity and inclusion. Diverse and inclusive leadership teams are more innovative and effective. Leaders will need to prioritise diversity and inclusion to drive organisational success.

Leaders must also embrace technology. Technology is transforming how leaders manage teams and make decisions. Leaders will need to be proficient in leveraging technology to enhance productivity and communication. Just look at the current impact of artificial intelligence (AI), and how this is exploding at a rapid rate. This means that agility and resilience, as well as having the ability to adapt quickly and remain resilient in the face of challenges, will be essential for future leaders. They will also need to have a view on sustainability and social responsibility and be able to prioritise sustainability and social responsibility in their future planning, recognising that long-term success is intertwined with the well-being of society and the environment.

Leadership is a dynamic and multi-faceted concept that plays a critical role in the success of any organisation. Effective leaders can inspire and motivate their teams, foster innovation and drive strategic goals. By understanding and leveraging the various aspects of leadership, organisations can create a positive and productive work environment that promotes growth and sustainability. Investing in leadership development, fostering a culture of innovation, and focusing on strategic planning and execution are key to building a robust leadership framework. As the business environment continues to evolve, leaders must remain adaptable, resilient and committed to continuous improvement to navigate the complexities of the modern world.

Understanding the inter-relationships between leadership, ideas, people and strategy provides a comprehensive framework for organisational success. By focusing on these interconnected elements, organisations can create a synergistic environment that drives innovation, efficiency and growth. Quite simply, leadership is a catalyst for change.

Great leadership – the catalyst for change

Winston Churchill is generally viewed as one of the great leaders of the past, primarily due to his steadfast resolve, inspiring rhetoric and strategic acumen during some of the most challenging times in modern history. As Prime Minister of the United Kingdom during World War II, he galvanised the British people with his powerful speeches and unyielding optimism, helping to maintain morale during the darkest days of the War.

Churchill's strategic decisions and diplomatic skills were crucial in forming and maintaining the Allied coalition, which ultimately led to the defeat of Nazi Germany. His ability to adapt, his deep understanding of history and politics, and his unwavering commitment to his nation's survival and freedom solidified his legacy as one of the most influential leaders of the 20th century.

Winston Churchill's leadership was a catalyst for change, particularly in the context of World War II and its aftermath. His decisive actions, passionate oratory and strategic vision brought about significant changes both during and after the war.

His public addresses – such as the 'We shall fight on the beaches' speech – played a crucial role in bolstering the morale of the British people, inspiring resilience and determination. His tactical military leadership was instrumental in coordinating the war effort, resulting in critical decisions that shaped the Allied strategy, and his insistence on continuing the fight against Nazi Germany after the fall of France was pivotal in the eventual Allied victory.

Churchill was a key figure in establishing and maintaining the Allied coalition, which included the United States and the Soviet Union. His relationships with leaders such as Franklin D. Roosevelt and Joseph Stalin were crucial in creating a united front against the Axis powers, and this helped Churchill play a significant role in shaping the post-war world. His advocacy for a united Europe and his warnings about the Iron Curtain and the threat of Soviet expansionism were influential in the development of NATO and the early stages of the Cold War.

While his domestic policies were more conservative, the war effort led to significant social changes in Britain, including the expansion of the welfare state. The experiences and demands of wartime Britain laid the groundwork for post-war reforms, such as the creation of the National Health Service. Churchill's leadership was thus not only a force for immediate wartime change, it also had lasting impacts on the global political landscape and British society.

Considering Churchill's example of leadership, we can safely say that leadership is the act of guiding and influencing others towards achieving a common goal. Effective leadership is crucial for fostering an environment where ideas can flourish, people feel valued and strategic goals are met. In essence, Churchill's leadership was a blend of inspirational communication, strategic acumen and a steadfast commitment to his principles, all underpinned by a resilient and charismatic personality – qualities that made him a pivotal figure during one of the most challenging periods in modern history.

Let's look at some other definitions and examples of leadership.

Leadership styles and their impact

There are many different leadership styles – transformational, transactional, democratic and autocratic, to name a few – that affect how ideas are generated and implemented, how people are motivated and managed, and how strategies are formulated and executed. Listed below are the more recognisable leadership styles.

> A. **Transformational leadership:** This style inspires and motivates employees to innovate and drive change. Leaders who adopt this style encourage creativity and are often at the forefront of implementing new ideas. These leaders foster an environment where new ideas are welcomed and employees feel empowered to take risks. Transformational leadership has been linked to higher levels of employee satisfaction, organisational commitment and performance.

Impacts transformational leaders have on teams include:

1. Encouraging a culture of innovation and continuous improvement.
2. Enhancing employee morale and job satisfaction.
3. Promoting loyalty and reducing turnover.

B. **Transactional leadership:** This focuses on structured tasks and rewards and can be effective in achieving short-term goals, although it may stifle innovation. Transactional leaders focus on routine, regimented activities and the maintenance of the status quo. They use rewards and punishments to motivate employees, which can be effective for achieving short-term goals and maintaining operational efficiency.

Impacts transactional leaders have on teams include:

1. Ensuring clarity regarding role and expectations.
2. Effectiveness in crisis situations where immediate action is required.
3. The risk of limiting creativity and long-term growth if overemphasised

C. **Democratic leadership**: This style of leadership involves team members in decision making, fostering a sense of ownership and collaboration. It is known for its inclusiveness and its ability to harness the diverse perspectives of team members.

Impacts democratic leaders have on teams include:

1. Fostering a collaborative and inclusive culture.
2. Higher levels of employee satisfaction and engagement.
3. The risk of slowing down decision-making processes due to the need for consensus.

D. **Autocratic leadership:** This style centralises decision-making authority, which can lead to quick decision making but may hinder creativity and employee engagement. Another term for this style of leadership is Authoritarian.

Impacts autocratic leaders have on teams include:

1. Enabling fast decision making and clear direction.
2. The possibility of lower employee morale and engagement.
3. Risk of stifling creativity and innovation.

Some other styles of leadership are referred to as Coaching, Affiliated, Coercive and Pacesetting.

Just as Churchill did with a nation, modern-day leaders provide a vision that guides an organisation's strategic direction. A clear, compelling vision not only aligns the organisation's goals but also inspires employees to contribute their best efforts.

A leader's style determines how they influence, motivate and direct their followers towards achieving set goals. According to research, the most effective leadership style is one that builds follower trust. When followers trust their leader, they are more likely to follow through with instructions, leading to goal accomplishment, while feeling able to freely air their ideas and suggestions.

Leadership style is usually a combination of the leader's personality, life experience, emotional intelligence, family dynamics and way of thinking. Understanding their own leadership style allows a leader to take ownership and control over and responsibility for the size and scope of tasks ahead. A *Harvard Business Review* study revealed that a manager's leadership style was responsible for 38% of a company's bottom-line profitability.

Effective leadership involves taking charge and knowing the appropriate leadership style for a particular situation. Flexibility based on changing circumstances leads to improved communication, collaboration, employee engagement and team effectiveness. Understanding your leadership style is key to becoming a more effective leader and achieving recognition within your organisation.

Who are the stakeholders in leadership?

It can be tough to keep track of your key stakeholders and the impact internal and external influences have on them. But effective stakeholder engagement is crucial for project success and organisational growth. Here are some best practices to enhance your stakeholder communications and successful interactions:

1. **Plan:** Start by creating a stakeholder engagement plan. Define who your stakeholders are, why you need to engage them, how you'll engage them and the desired outcomes.
2. **Define your stakeholder list:** Identify all individuals, groups and organisations affected by or influencing your project or organisation. This comprehensive list will guide your engagement efforts and helps tailor messages and methods for specific stakeholders.
3. **Prioritise key stakeholders:** Not all stakeholders require the same level of engagement. Segment them based on influence, interest and impact. Focus on key stakeholders – those critical to your project's success – while still broadly engaging others.
4. **Tailor communication:** Customise your messages to resonate with different stakeholder groups. Acknowledge their unique needs, concerns and perspectives to build trust and understanding.
5. **Inclusivity matters:** Ensure that all groups can participate in engagement activities. Use diverse channels to gather feedback and involve stakeholders.
6. **Listen actively:** Engage in two-way communication. Listen to stakeholder feedback and acknowledge their insights. Let their input shape decisions and project direction.
7. **Provide regular updates:** Keep stakeholders informed through consistent communication. Use email newsletters, social media or dedicated websites to share project progress.

8. **Collaborate and discuss:** Create opportunities for collaboration. Conduct workshops, focus groups or one-on-one meetings. Encourage dialogue and foster a sense of ownership among stakeholders.

Remember, effective stakeholder engagement builds trust, aligns goals and contributes to successful project outcomes.

Eight ways to build gravitas

Gravitas, or dignity, is an important yet invisible aspect of business that can make a significant difference to how you are perceived. It's the seriousness and importance of manner that inspires feelings of respect and trust in others – especially if you are just joining a new company.

Starting a new role can be daunting, but here are my top eight suggestions to help you build gravitas and momentum:

1. Greet everyone across the business and interview key players in your team regarding their roles and responsibilities.
2. Review and reconnoitre the facilities and assets of the business.
3. Develop an action list of urgent business-critical issues to resolve first.
4. Display the organisation's values around the facility and test team members' beliefs about them.
5. Introduce new meeting systems and documents to monitor performance and development of team members.
6. Test the vision and mission statements with team members, customers and suppliers to get feedback.
7. Develop appraisal formats that encompass the strategic plan and team members' actions towards delivery.
8. Create a story and theme to unify the business.

Remember, the tone of change is crucial when developing gravitas in your new role. Read the audience and ensure that your communication style suits the environment.

Set specific goals, so you deliver on the invisible element of gravitas in your role.

Six leadership tests/refreshers

I've talked in the past about self-actualising being the best version of yourself as a leader. Leading on from that, I want to share some tests, or refreshers, to put yourself through regularly to stay on track with your leadership self-development journey.

Leadership test/refresher 1

In the realm of leadership, strategic vision and purpose serve as the cornerstones of transformational leadership. Leaders who possess a clear vision and purpose inspire and motivate their teams to achieve extraordinary results. Having a compelling vision of the future is crucial for effective leadership. A vision is a forward-looking, inspiring view of what an organisation or team aims to achieve.

> A compelling vision goes beyond the leader's personal view – it resonates with the hopes and dreams of the team. Being forward-looking and being able to envision exciting possibilities distinguishes leaders from non-leaders. It helps leaders make decisions about where to focus resources, how to allocate efforts and which goals to pursue. Without a clear vision, strategy development lacks purpose and coherence.
>
> When a leader shares a vision and goal with their team, it inspires collective effort. Team members understand their roles in achieving the vision, fostering alignment and commitment. A shared vision motivates individuals to work together towards a common purpose.
>
> The vision statement communicates an organisation's purpose to stakeholders. It serves as a beacon, guiding actions and decisions. Together with the mission, the vision informs goals and objectives, ensuring that the strategy stays on track.

Vision and strategy are essential for effective leadership. A well-crafted vision inspires, guides and aligns teams, leading to extraordinary outcomes.

So now, take the test!

Hand on your heart, as a leader – CEO, MD, GM or any other type of leader in any size business – circle Yes/No for the things you do regularly – and I mean regularly. To coin a phrase, like a broken record on repeat.

- Develop a clear and compelling company vision with input from other senior leaders. **YES/NO**
- Collaborate with the CFO to align financial goals with strategic objectives. **YES/NO**
- Ensure your strategic plan incorporates financial perspectives for sustainable growth. **YES/NO**
- Regularly review and update the strategic plan based on company performance. **YES/NO**
- Ensure company-wide understanding of and alignment with strategic objectives. **YES/NO**
- Evaluate the impact of industry trends and changes on the company's strategy. **YES/NO**
- Communicate the vision and strategy to all stakeholders. **YES/NO**

Leadership test/refresher 2

The relationships between leadership and culture and leadership and talent management are crucial for organisational success. Organisational culture refers to the collection of values, beliefs, assumptions and norms that guide behaviour and mindset within an organisation.

Effective leaders ensure alignment with the organisation's mission, purpose and vision. They communicate these foundational elements to employees, emphasising how their daily work contributes to overall success. When leaders foster a positive culture, it motivates employees, enhances collaboration and impacts performance.

Company culture directly affects talent management in several ways. Firstly, culture attracts top talent and encourages employee engagement. Engaged employees are more likely to perform at their best and stay committed to the organisation. A strong culture fosters a sense of belonging and purpose among employees, leading to higher job satisfaction and retention rates. When employees feel aligned with the organisation's values and vision, they are more productive and contribute more effectively.

Leaders can establish a talent-first culture by prioritising talent management. This approach recognises that having the right skills and capabilities is essential for implementing ideas and achieving organisational goals. By putting talent first, companies improve performance and gain a competitive advantage.

So, effective leadership shapes organisational culture which, in turn, impacts talent management outcomes. Cultivating a positive culture enhances employee satisfaction, productivity and retention, ultimately contributing to overall success.

Now, take the second test!

The same rules apply as before – keep your answers honest and circle Yes/No for the things you do *regularly*.

- Work with senior leaders to define and execute a talent management strategy. **YES/NO**
- Foster employee development and career progression. **YES/NO**
- Develop and foster collaboration across departments. **YES/NO**
- Recognise and reward performance. **YES/NO**
- Partner with the finance teams to set financial ethics standards. **YES/NO**
- Foster an environment supporting creativity and innovation. **YES/NO**
- Prioritise a customer-centric approach in all strategic planning. **YES/NO**

- Promote open communication across
  the organisation. **YES/NO**
- Champion team building and collaborative efforts. **YES/NO**
- Strive for a work environment that encourages
  innovation. **YES/NO**
- Implement strategies for succession planning. **YES/NO**
- Maintain a balance of team skills and experience. **YES/NO**
- Foster a continuous learning and professional
  development program. **YES/NO**

Leadership test/refresher 3

Leadership plays a crucial role in maintaining brand reputation and business continuity, especially during challenging times. As a leader, your actions significantly impact your organisation's trustworthiness and stakeholders' confidence.

Upholding values, fostering unity and ensuring transparency are key elements in building a strong brand and operational continuity. Take the test and evaluate your leadership practices. Regularly assess whether you:

- Act as the face of the company in public forums. **YES/NO**
- Manage reputation risks effectively. **YES/NO**
- Engage with stakeholders to maintain positive
  brand perception. **YES/NO**
- Review and update business continuity plans. **YES/NO**
- Establish succession plans and develop
  internal talent. **YES/NO**
- Communicate plans to stakeholders and maintain
  a strong company narrative. **YES/NO**
- Mitigate risks for operational continuity. **YES/NO**

Leadership test/refresher 4

The interplay between operational and financial efficiency is crucial for the success of any organisation.

For me, operational efficiency refers to how well an organisation utilises its resources (such as labour, technology and processes) to produce goods or services. It focuses on streamlining processes, reducing waste and improving productivity. An easy example to visualise is a manufacturing company that reduces production time, minimises defects and optimises inventory management, thus demonstrating operational efficiency.

Financial efficiency relates to how well an organisation manages its financial resources to achieve its goals. It involves optimising financial processes, managing cash flow and maximising profitability. Financial efficiency aims to maximise profits by controlling costs, increasing revenue opportunities and managing financial risks. Not to mention working capital management. A company that efficiently manages its cash flow, minimises debt and invests wisely demonstrates financial efficiency. Sounds easy, right?

Improving operational efficiency often leads to better financial performance – and vice versa. Good organisations strike a balance. For example, investing in new technology (operational efficiency) may require upfront costs but can lead to long-term financial gains.

So now, take the test/refresher! Circle Yes/No for the things you do regularly when it comes to operational and financial efficiency.

- Partner with the finance team to identify potential financial and operational risks and implement mitigation strategies. **YES/NO**

- Implement systems and processes that optimise productivity. **YES/NO**

- Monitor operational performance and implement improvement strategies. **YES/NO**

- Foster a culture of continuous improvement. **YES/NO**
- Invest in technology and tools that improve efficiency. **YES/NO**
- Develop strategies to manage supply chain effectively. **YES/NO**
- Address operational issues promptly. **YES/NO**
- Directly interface with the CFO to oversee the company's financial health, including budgeting and cash flow management. **YES/NO**
- Make key decisions on capital expenditure, investments, and risk management. **YES/NO**
- Develop robust financial reporting and auditing processes in collaboration with the CFO. **YES/NO**
- Regularly review financial performance against targets, adjusting strategies as needed. **YES/NO**
- Implement strategies to optimise cost efficiency. **YES/NO**
- Ensure compliance with industry financial regulations and reporting standards. **YES/NO**

Leadership test/refresher 5

In this refresher/test, I wanted to delve into the interplay between corporate governance and risk management from a leadership perspective.

Risk management is central to corporate governance. Over the years, the corporate world has witnessed various risk failures (such as the financial crisis of 2008) and technological advancements that brought both opportunities and massive risks. In response, corporations adopted new, more transparent practices to manage risk. These practices now fall under the umbrella of governance, risk and compliance (GRC).

The role of risk management in corporate governance is to inform how corporations and their boards operate concerning risk. It involves considering the risk exposure of every business activity and implementing practices such as due diligence, internal controls and more to manage risk proactively.

As risk management influences corporate governance, modern governance has introduced new risk management practices where many boards now prioritise smarter risk-taking, backed by the assurances that corporate governance provides.

When good corporate governance is in place, corporations can proactively identify and mitigate risk, reducing their risk exposure and ultimately limiting reputational and financial damage.

Now, take the test/refresher. Circle Yes/No for the things you do regularly when it comes to corporate governance and risk management.

- Collaborate with your COO and CFO, or Senior Executives, to ensure robust corporate governance. **YES/NO**
- Ensure accurate financial reporting, regulatory compliance, internal controls and procedures for preventing fraud. **YES/NO**
- Ensure the company's activities align with its mission and values, working closely with all department heads. **YES/NO**
- Maintain transparency in all operations and reporting. **YES/NO**
- Manage company policies and corporate legal affairs. **YES/NO**
- Foster a culture of ethical conduct across the organisation. **YES/NO**
- Partner with the finance team to identify potential financial and operational risks and implement mitigation strategies. **YES/NO**
- Monitor risk exposure and respond promptly to risk events. **YES/NO**
- Establish a robust risk management framework. **YES/NO**
- Regularly review risk management policies and procedures. **YES/NO**

- Ensure risk considerations are integrated into
  decision-making processes.   **YES/NO**
- Communicate risk management practices
  to stakeholders.   **YES/NO**

<u>Leadership test/refresher 6</u>

Let's face it, if I of all people have to browbeat you about customer focus and stakeholder management as a leader then you have some serious issues. But guess what? There are still people out there who don't get it. We are not all perfect, so the good thing is we can have little lists like this that can assist. I did a recent post on who stakeholders are, but just as a reminder, stakeholders include investors, employees, customers, suppliers, communities, and governments. Their interests shape the organisation's decisions and outcomes.

So now, take the test/refresher! Circle Yes/No for the things you do regularly when it comes to customer and stakeholder management.

- Develop strategies to improve customer satisfaction.   **YES/NO**
- Foster a customer-centric culture.   **YES/NO**
- Collaborate with the finance, product and marketing
  leaders to ensure company products
  are financially viable.   **YES/NO**
- Regularly gather and analyse customer feedback.   **YES/NO**
- Ensure products or services meet customer needs.   **YES/NO**
- Implement effective customer relationship
  management strategies.   **YES/NO**
- Engage directly with customers to understand
  their needs and concerns.   **YES/NO**
- Identify key stakeholders in the company's
  environment and prioritise based on influence/interest.   **YES/NO**
- Maintain positive relationships with all stakeholders.   **YES/NO**

- Foster a culture of responsibility towards stakeholders. **YES/NO**
- Ensure strategies create value for stakeholders. **YES/NO**
- Regularly engage with stakeholders to understand their concerns and expectations. **YES/NO**
- Implement effective communication mechanisms to gather stakeholder feedback. **YES/NO**
- Ensure transparency in communications with all internal and external stakeholders. **YES/NO**
- Implement strategies to manage stakeholder conflicts. **YES/NO**
- Regularly report on company performance to stakeholders. **YES/NO**

Now take the *total* leadership test:

- Results – if you get between:
  - 0-50% – Back to the drawing board
  - 50-70% – Getting there but need more focus
  - 70 – 90% – Almost a leadership legend
  - 100% – Supersonic and a leadership legend

The Total Leadership Test

- Develop a clear and compelling company vision with input from other senior leaders. **YES/NO**
- Collaborate with the CFO to align financial goals with strategic objectives. **YES/NO**
- Ensure strategic plan incorporates financial perspectives for sustainable growth. **YES/NO**
- Regularly review and update the strategic plan based on company performance. **YES/NO**
- Ensure company-wide understanding and alignment with strategic objectives. **YES/NO**

- Evaluate the impact of industry trends and changes on the company's strategy. **YES/NO**
- Communicate the vision and strategy to all stakeholders. **YES/NO**
- Work with senior leaders to define and execute a talent management strategy. **YES/NO**
- Foster employee development and career progression. **YES/NO**
- Develop and foster collaboration across departments. **YES/NO**
- Recognise and reward performance. **YES/NO**
- Partner with the finance teams to set financial ethics standards. **YES/NO**
- Foster an environment supporting creativity and innovation. **YES/NO**
- Prioritise a customer-centric approach in all strategic planning. **YES/NO**
- Promote open communication across the organisation. **YES/NO**
- Champion team building and collaborative efforts. **YES/NO**
- Strive for a work environment that encourages innovation. **YES/NO**
- Implement strategies for succession planning. **YES/NO**
- Maintain a balance of team skills and experience. **YES/NO**
- Foster a continuous learning and professional development program. **YES/NO**
- Act as the face of the company in public forums. **YES/NO**
- Manage reputation risks effectively. **YES/NO**
- Engage with stakeholders to maintain a positive brand perception. **YES/NO**
- Review and update business continuity plans. **YES/NO**

- Establish succession plans and develop internal talent. **YES/NO**
- Communicate plans to stakeholders and maintain a strong company narrative. **YES/NO**
- Mitigate risks for operational continuity. **YES/NO**
- Partner with the finance team to identify risks and implement mitigation strategies. **YES/NO**
- Implement systems and processes that optimise productivity. **YES/NO**
- Monitor operational performance and implement improvement strategies. **YES/NO**
- Foster a culture of continuous improvement. **YES/NO**
- Invest in technology and tools that improve efficiency. **YES/NO**
- Develop strategies to manage supply chain effectively. **YES/NO**
- Address operational and issues promptly. **YES/NO**
- Interface with the CFO to oversee the company's financial health, budgeting and cash flow. **YES/NO**
- Make key decisions on capital expenditure, investments and risk management. **YES/NO**
- Develop robust financial reporting and auditing processes in collaboration with the CFO **YES/NO**
- Regularly review financial performance against targets adjusting strategies as needed. **YES/NO**
- Implement strategies to optimise cost efficiency. **YES/NO**
- Ensure compliance with industry financial regulations and reporting standards. **YES/NO**
- Collaborate with your COO and CFO, or senior executives, to ensure robust corporate governance. **YES/NO**
- Ensure accurate reporting, regulatory compliance, controls and procedures for preventing fraud. **YES/NO**

- Ensure company's activities align with its mission and values, working closely with all department heads. **YES/NO**
- Maintain transparency in all operations and reporting. **YES/NO**
- Manage company policies and corporate legal affairs. **YES/NO**
- Foster a culture of ethical conduct across the organisation. **YES/NO**
- With finance, identify potential financial operational risks and implement mitigation strategies. **YES/NO**
- Monitor risk exposure and respond promptly to risk events. **YES/NO**
- Establish a robust risk management framework. **YES/NO**
- Regularly review risk management policies and procedures. **YES/NO**
- Ensure risk considerations are integrated into decision-making processes. **YES/NO**
- Communicate risk management practices to stakeholders. **YES/NO**
- Develop strategies to improve customer satisfaction. **YES/NO**
- Foster a customer-centric culture. **YES/NO**
- Collaborate with internal leaders to ensure company products are financially viable. **YES/NO**
- Regularly gather and analyse customer feedback. **YES/NO**
- Ensure products or services meet customer needs. **YES/NO**
- Implement effective customer relationship management strategies. **YES/NO**
- Engage directly with customers to understand their needs and concerns. **YES/NO**
- Identify key stakeholders in the company's environment and prioritise based on influence/ interest. **YES/NO**
- Maintain positive relationships with all stakeholders. **YES/NO**

- Foster a culture of responsibility towards stakeholders. **YES/NO**
- Ensure strategies create value for stakeholders. **YES/NO**
- Regularly engage with stakeholders to understand their concerns and expectations. **YES/NO**
- Implement effective communication mechanisms to gather stakeholder feedback. **YES/NO**
- Ensure transparency in communications with all internal and external stakeholders. **YES/NO**
- Implement strategies to manage stakeholder conflicts. **YES/NO**
- Regularly report on company performance to stakeholders. **YES/NO**

SCORE: _____ **/69 =** _____ **% Self Rating**

What areas should I improve in or start to do?

_____
_____
_____
_____
_____
_____
_____
_____
_____
_____
_____
_____
_____

Good role models

I was reading a post from a connection on LinkedIn who mentioned his experience as a father. It struck a chord with me – not that I don't understand that fatherhood is profound, but reflecting on it, it's important to understand how important role models are. They demonstrate responsibility, integrity and compassion. Just as CEOs influence company culture, parents shape family dynamics and values. Mothers and fathers provide emotional, social and spiritual protection. Their affection, discipline and guidance contribute to a child's well-being and character development. Like good leaders, parents encourage competition and independence. They emphasise conceptual communication, expanding their children's vocabulary and intellectual capacities. Putting on my leadership and coaching hat, I'd suggest that exemplary CEOs and leaders combine the reality of what they ought to do in their roles with who they are as human beings. They deliberately choose how to behave based on questions such as:

- What legacy do I want to leave?
- What do I want others to say about me as a leader?
- What do I stand for?

Good leaders understand that authenticity matters. They lead with integrity, transparency and a genuine commitment to their values. By doing so, they inspire trust, foster collaboration and create a positive organisational culture. Why is this important? There is a difference between good and poor leaders and the future of employees' development and success – which ultimately becomes yours. A good leader welcomes employee suggestions, actively listens and encourages open communication. They recognise that feedback is essential. A challenged leader feels bothered by employee input, dismisses ideas or criticises without understanding, stifling creativity and discouraging team members from contributing.

Positive role models embrace tough questions, appreciate diverse perspectives and encourage critical thinking. They see challenges as opportunities for growth, whereas poor leaders react defensively, avoid difficult questions or suppress dissent. This behaviour limits progress and stifles creativity. Today, great leadership values diversity, promotes inclusion and leverages different strengths. True leaders create environments where everyone feels respected and valued. They lead by example, actively participate and support the team. They understand that leadership isn't just about delegating. They don't avoid getting hands-on, nor do they disconnect from day-to-day realities. A great role model recognises and nurtures talent, provides growth opportunities and celebrates team members' achievements.

In summary, good leaders inspire, empower and drive positive change, while poor leaders can create toxicity and hinder growth. Mothers and fathers play a critical leadership role by nurturing their families and leaving lasting impressions on future generations.

Thanks for the inspiration, Tim, and keep enjoying fatherhood and all the great stuff that comes with it.

Leading with a passion for people's success

Being a positive and effective leader means addressing workplace challenges and toxic behaviours that are culture killers, so you can maintain a healthy work environment. Let's explore some strategies to address seven key issues that exist in today's busy workplace:

1. **Micromanagement**
    - Recognise the signs: Recognise micromanagement by observing excessive scrutiny, lack of autonomy and constant supervision.
    - Initiate communication: Request a meeting with the micromanager to discuss your concerns.

- **Ask for clarity:** Understand expectations and minimise the need for constant supervision by clarifying tasks and processes.
- **Demonstrate competence:** Prove your abilities and build trust.
- **Seek support:** Reach out to colleagues or mentors for advice and encouragement.

2. Unrealistic expectations

- **Set clear expectations:** Communicate openly with your supervisor about what is feasible and achievable.
- **Prioritise tasks:** Focus on high-impact tasks and manage expectations regarding timelines.
- **Negotiate:** If expectations are unrealistic, discuss alternative solutions or adjustments.

3. Blame culture

- **Switch to a learning mindset:** Encourage open sharing of mistakes and focus on learning rather than blame.
- **Systems approach:** Instead of blaming individuals, analyse where the process broke down.
- **Promote kindness:** Recognise that negative experiences can have a stronger impact than positive ones, so be kind in your interactions.

4. Lack of empathy

- **Connect with others:** Take time to understand co-workers on a personal level.
- **Listen actively:** Show genuine interest in their feelings and perspectives.
- **Avoid stereotyping:** Treat everyone as an individual with unique needs.

5. **Lack of support**
   - Support yourself: Develop self-reliance and positive coping mechanisms.
   - Ask for support: Communicate transparently with co-workers and supervisors about your needs.
   - Regular communication: Discuss work problems and address them collaboratively.

6. **Self-entitlement**
   - Recognise beliefs: Understand common entitled employee beliefs and set clear expectations.
   - Model humility: Demonstrate hard work, flexibility and a willingness to learn.

7. **Incivility**
   - Lead by example: Model respectful behaviour and kindness.
   - Address incidents promptly: If you witness incivility, address it quickly and professionally.
   - Set boundaries: Establish clear guidelines for respectful interactions.

Remember, creating a positive workplace culture requires collective effort. By addressing challenges proactively, you contribute to a healthier and more productive environment – but, more importantly, you are demonstrating a focused leadership approach for the individual's success.

Leading like a rhino
Recently, I had the pleasure of leading a training session with a team of young, bold and impressive professionals. Despite their ages, they were excelling in their fields and had a thirst for knowledge, constantly asking 'why' throughout the session. Even as a more experienced professional, it was challenging at times to discuss points on leadership, but it was also inspiring to witness their incredible confidence and curiosity.

To make the session more collaborative and fun, I introduced an icebreaker exercise where each participant chose an animal that best represented their selling and work style. We then discussed the leadership attributes of each animal, with the top five being the lion, cheetah, tiger, elephant and rhino. After voting, the rhino emerged as the winner, with the loudest voice and rhino's advocate in the room wearing an 'Ecko Unlimited' T-shirt! To the group, the rhino represented confidence, authority and power/force, and they identified ten leadership attributes that their rhinos and great leaders share.

It was a great reminder that leadership comes in all shapes and sizes and that we can learn from professionals of all ages and backgrounds.

Here are ten metaphorical leadership attributes of a rhino:

- **Strength:** Rhinos possess immense physical strength, symbolising resilience and the ability to overcome challenges.
- **Tenacity:** Their determination to move forward mirrors a leader's persistence in pursuing goals despite obstacles.
- **Protectiveness:** Rhinos are known for being fiercely protective of their young, reflecting a leader's duty to safeguard their team.
- **Grounded:** With their heavy bodies and strong presence, rhinos symbolise stability and reliability in decision making.
- **Focus:** Rhinos have a clear sense of direction, representing a leader's ability to maintain focus on their vision.
- **Adaptability:** Rhinos can thrive in various environments, akin to a leader's capacity to adjust strategies in changing circumstances.
- **Courage:** Their willingness to confront threats head-on exemplifies the bravery required in leadership roles.
- **Introspection:** Rhinos often appear calm and contemplative, symbolising the importance of self-reflection in effective leadership.

- **Collaboration:** While generally solitary, rhinos can engage in social behaviours, illustrating the value of teamwork and collaboration.
- **Legacy:** Rhinos play a crucial role in their ecosystems, highlighting a leader's impact on the community and the importance of leaving a legacy.

Ten qualities of a great leader

If you were asked to define strategic leadership, what would you say? While there may not be a definitive business definition, to me it's about understanding the landscape you're operating in and leading with passion. As social beings, we need each other to drive change and transformation at a personal level, and strategic leadership does that on many different levels.

Here are 10 principles of strategic leadership that I'd like to share. These are soft skills that can be developed to head in the direction of good strategic leadership:

1. Always bring your best self to work. Don't hold back.
2. Make it safe to fail.
3. Be transparent, open and honest about information and feedback.
4. Hire for change and transformation.
5. Allow and create multiple paths for raising and testing new ideas.
6. Distribute workflows and business streams responsibly.
7. Always look for opportunities for experience-based learning.
8. Provide access and exposure to other strategists.
9. Ongoing personal leadership development is critical.
10. Reflection time is a must, so set aside quality time.

Master these eight skills

Mastering the following eight skills can also contribute to becoming a great strategic leader quickly:

1. Being patient
2. Being consistent
3. Managing your time
4. Listening wisely
5. Having confidence
6. Not whining
7. Being able to speak up
8. Knowing yourself

Remember, you are on a self-development journey with the discipline of a samurai warrior. Keep learning and growing as a leader.

What is extreme leadership?

Leadership is a crucial element in driving success in any organisation, and retired US Navy Officer, author and podcaster Jocko Willink's TEDx talk on extreme leadership and ownership is a must-watch for anyone looking to lead (you can access the talk by scanning the QR code at the end of this section). His talk emphasises the importance of accountability, decentralising command and placing trust in others to perform. Willink's message is clear – there are no bad teams, only bad leaders.

Willink's talk is full of valuable lessons that can be applied across various aspects of life. He stresses the importance of checking your ego, being accountable for your own actions, and having a deep belief in what you do. He also emphasises the importance of planning, decisiveness and discipline.

The lessons Willink learned during his time in the forces allowed him to see humanity in a radical way – through the brutality of war, it came down to the core elements of living or dying-survival. This experience allowed him to take ownership of his life and helped him lead himself to victory.

As we plan for a successful future, investing in team members who take ownership of themselves and the problems they face is critical. Remember, extreme ownership comes from practice and always taking the lead.

Scan this QR code to access Jocko Willink's TEDx talk on extreme leadership

Five signs of courage in leadership

Some time ago, I had a discussion with an old colleague about leadership and its impact on team members. We agreed that it's essential to avoid bad habits from poor leadership and focus on what real courage looks like in leadership. Here are the key takeaways:

1. A courageous leader embraces unfamiliar solutions, giving their team members the confidence to join them on the journey.
2. Letting go of the controls and allowing others to make decisions while still maintaining responsibility shows faith and trust and also allows team members to lead. Changing course from the original flight plan is okay, because recognising when the trajectory is off and shifting to deal with issues or errors is a sign of a great leader.

3. A courageous leader doesn't ignore the elephant in the room but deals with the real issues that lead to a better tomorrow.
4. Reconstructing achievement is all about courageous leadership admitting that what gave us success today may not give us success tomorrow.

So, take on the courageous leader challenge and never look back.

The GARY Principle

Creating a leadership and learning culture in your organisation is not easy, but it's essential for long-term success. The 'GARY Principle' is a good basis for developing this in your workplace. What does it stand for?

G. Growth mindset: Encourage a growth mindset within your team. This means fostering an environment where employees believe their abilities can be developed through dedication and hard work. Leaders should model this mindset by continuously seeking personal and professional growth.

A. Accountability: Establish a culture of accountability. Leaders and team members should take responsibility for their actions and outcomes. This builds trust and ensure that everyone is committed to the organisation's goals.

R. Recognition: Recognise and reward achievements and efforts. Celebrating successes, both big and small, motivates employees and reinforces positive behaviours. Recognition can be formal, like awards, or informal, like a simple thank you.

Y. Yearning for Learning: Cultivate a yearning for learning. Encourage continuous education and development through training programs, workshops and other learning opportunities. Leaders should also be learners, demonstrating that learning is a lifelong journey. Balancing these elements helps create a dynamic and supportive environment where leadership and learning thrive together.

A culture that prioritises both leadership development and continuous learning drives innovation and employee engagement and attracts top talent. Here are some essential components of a strong leadership and learning culture:

1. **Leadership development:** Leaders should model the behaviours they want to see in their teams, demonstrate empathy and adaptability, and encourage a growth mindset. Providing coaching and mentorship opportunities fosters a sense of purpose and develops leadership skills.
2. **Continuous learning:** Tailor learning experiences to individual needs; offer a mix of formal training, on-the-job learning and self-directed resources. Encourage knowledge sharing among colleagues through forums, workshops and peer learning circles.

Strategies for cultivating a leadership and learning culture include:

1. Set a clear vision for the organisation's growth and communicate the importance of both leadership development and learning.
2. Empower employees by involving them in co-designing learning programs and providing autonomy in choosing learning paths and resources.
3. Allocate resources to support leadership programs and continuous learning.
4. Demonstrate leadership by actively participating in learning activities, showing vulnerability by admitting mistakes and sharing lessons learned.

5. Create an environment where employees feel safe to take risks, ask questions and share ideas; encourage experimentation and celebrate learning from failures.
6. Measure the impact of employee engagement, retention and skill development.

Cultivating a leadership and learning culture requires commitment, resources and alignment from top leadership. By investing in both leadership development and continuous learning, organisations can thrive in an ever-changing world and deliver on their promise of deep cultural change and being a great place to work.

The management skills matrix

In my downtime recently, I revisited a book gifted to me by my brother over a decade ago. The author, J.R. Wooden, was a legendary basketball coach who created a pyramid of success that turned individual players into unstoppable teams. His philosophy was simple: "Success is peace of mind which is a direct result of self-satisfaction in knowing you did your best to become the best that you are capable of becoming."

Inspired by this philosophy, I decided to create my own management skills and strategy matrix. I realised that there is a strong correlation between strategy, leadership skills and the ability to navigate through the unpredictable terrain of the competitive landscape. It's essential to identify the attributes and actions that will help you achieve your goals and aspirations.

To achieve success, it's important to consider Maslow's 'Hierarchy of Needs', which works symbiotically with leadership capabilities and strategic skills. I believe that by developing a strong foundation of management skills and strategy, we can all become the best versions of ourselves.

The concept of VUCA

As a CEO, general manager, business owner or leader, it can feel like you're constantly putting out fires in your business. Economic factors such as inflation, supply chain issues and staff retention can make it challenging to navigate the next steps of your strategic plan. In addition, ongoing impacts of COVID from team members and organisations navigating hybrid and back-to-work arrangements can result in unwanted experiences where morale and staff sensitivity become greater issues than ever before, creating an environment that's **V**olatile, **U**ncertain, **C**omplex and **A**mbiguous – or 'VUCA' for short.

So, how can you climb out of this environment and become a great business model? By focusing on key areas such as loyalty of customers, stock availability, well-trained staff, speed of fulfilment, the in-store/business experience, personalisation and sustainability.

It's all about practicing how well you can predict the results of your actions and how much information you gather to navigate the situations unfolding before you. Staff training, communication and business development are essential to successfully navigate the VUCA environment.

Remember, directing your precious team resources towards these areas can help you come out the other side winning.

From VUCA to VUCAAC

Is this the new abnormal? VUCA has certainly become a part of our professional lives. But have you heard of VUCAAC? It stands for **V**ibrant, **U**nreal, **C**razy, **A**mazing, **A**doring and **C**reative and reflects how fast changes and situations evolve before us today. In a VUCA world, you cannot sit around and wait. You need to do everything with speed and intent and by clearly defining your purpose and focus.

Transformational change fails because a clear picture of the future is not painted to the end users. Sharing what is happening now and impacting people's futures is one of the most important aspects of transparent leadership. Most leaders who start the process of change adapt, improvise and refine processes to overcome VUCA. Leaders need to know what to change and need to understand and exploit their company's superpower and those of its team to make a mark.

Here are seven tips to master the art of VUCAAC:

1. Active listening
2. Caring and demanding leadership
3. Creativity
4. Customer love
5. Emotional sensibility
6. Speedy executional excellence
7. Technology mastery

More importantly, master these abilities in this time of VUCA and you will master your VUCAAC. Remember, becoming the purveyor of hope by changing VUCA to represent Vibrant, Unreal, Crazy, Amazing, Adoring and Creative is key to success.

Creativity in leadership

Great leadership is about creativity. A good definition of creativity is 'seeing what everyone else has seen and thinking what no one else has thought'. Creative leaders unleash their minds to conceive innovative ideas, while innovative leaders introduce change to make those ideas viable. Both are incredibly good.

Curiosity is a trait of a creative leader. A curious leader has lots of ideas and is constantly reframing. Creativity takes courage because it fights against institutional thinking and what we think is the norm. It is one of the most significant game-changing factors for modern leaders to possess in a turbulent world.

As professionals, we want to be with people who are creative, love what they do and have an edge. Creativity ignites enthusiasm and energy, which are essential in solving problems and addressing the competitive landscape.

Ask yourself, what is your next move and how can you be more creative when making it? Life can be like a chess game, so here are some tips for you to liberate your thinking and become more creative.

Here are five tips for liberating your thinking in creative leadership. As mentioned, it like a game of chess.

1. **Pawn: Embrace Incremental Change**

   Just as pawns can gradually advance across the board, start with small, manageable changes in your approach. Encourage your team to propose incremental ideas that can lead to significant innovations over time. Every small step can contribute to a larger strategy, reinforcing the idea that creativity doesn't always require grand gestures.

2. **Knight: Think Outside the Box**

   The knight's unique L-shaped movement represents the importance of unconventional thinking. As a leader, challenge yourself to approach problems from different angles. Foster a culture where diverse perspectives are valued, allowing team members to explore creative solutions that might not follow traditional paths.

3. **Bishop: Leverage Your Vision**

   Bishops move diagonally across the board, symbolising the ability to see opportunities others might miss. Cultivate a visionary mindset by staying attuned to trends and shifts in your industry. Encourage your team to look beyond the obvious and explore innovative directions, using insights to inspire creative strategies.

4. **Rook: Build Strong Foundations**

   Rooks are powerful and steadfast, moving freely along ranks and files. Establish a solid foundation of trust and open communication within your team. A strong team dynamic fosters a safe environment for sharing ideas and taking creative risks. Encourage collaboration, which can lead to unexpected and innovative outcomes.

5. **Queen: Be Bold and Versatile**

   The queen is the most powerful piece on the board, able to move in any direction. As a leader, embody versatility and boldness in your decision making. Encourage your team to experiment and take calculated risks. Show that creativity is not just about having ideas but also about the courage to implement them and adapt when necessary.

By incorporating these chess-inspired strategies, you can liberate your thinking and enhance your creative leadership.

Being resilient, overcoming setbacks and driving trust

Leadership is all about mastering the three abilities that are crucial in today's business world. To become a more creative-thinking leader, you must learn to be resilient, overcome setbacks and drive trust. These abilities are sequential and have a symbiotic relationship with each other. Reframing challenges from a different perspective and using the power of positive emotions can help you boost a sense of belonging and accomplishment, which will invigorate your ideas for a more purposeful life.

Physical activities can supercharge your reduction in stress and excite the brain into a positive mindset, leading to working closely with trusted networks of people you know. If you don't have any trusted networks, now is the time to get out of your comfort zone and build some.

Identifying your signature strengths is crucial to building up these three abilities. Doing a Gallup strengths finder can help you find your top five strengths to get you going. Using your strengths to develop these abilities will give you more control, confidence, and a positive future no matter what arises.

Check out the graphic I created that shows the attributes of each ability.

Daily principles to live by

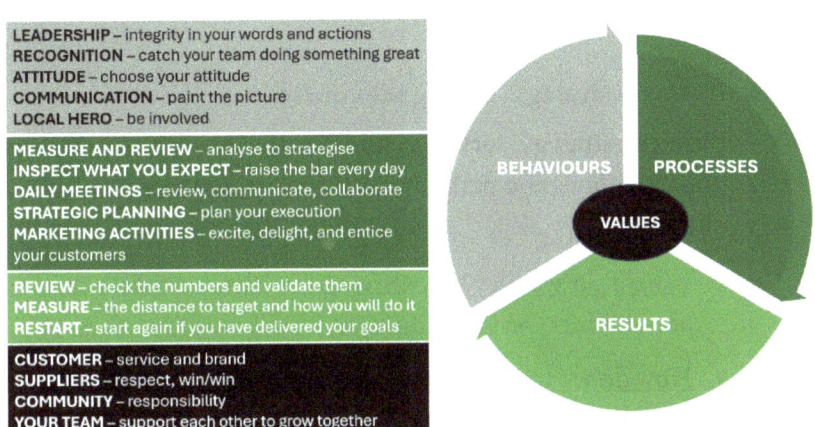

As a seasoned manager, it's surprising to find oneself at a loss when it comes to making improvements in the workplace. But where to start? This was the question posed to me by a new manager I spoke with recently.

I reminded them that understanding key metrics for success was important, but adopting a disciplined approach to building an action plan was critical. I shared a template and four key points, including comments around regular one-on-ones and formal documentation, self-diagnosis and co-created action plans, connecting performance objectives to the appraisal process, and formal training where applicable.

I'm happy to say they graciously accepted the advice, and I urged them to then define principles for their team and create shared accountability for future success. The graphic illustrates what we came up with, to get the process going. Ask yourself: What principles have worked for me in the past?

The interplay of business strategy, leadership and people

I have always had a bias about one thing in business. It's that in the dynamic landscape of business, success hinges on the delicate interplay between three critical elements: business strategy, leadership and people. These components are not isolated, rather, they form an intricate web that shapes organisational outcomes. This is how they synergise to drive excellence.

1. **Business strategy: setting the course**

   Business strategy serves as the North Star for any organisation. It defines the path forward, answering three fundamental questions:

   - Where do we play? Identifying markets, customer segments and product/service offerings.

   - How do we win? Crafting competitive advantages, differentiation and value propositions.

   - What are our long-term goals? Setting clear objectives and milestones.

   A robust business strategy provides direction, aligns resources and guides decision making. However, strategy alone remains inert without effective execution.

2. **Leadership: the catalyst for action**

   Effective leaders are not just managers; they are architects of change, orchestrating the execution of strategic intent. They breathe life into strategy, transforming abstract plans into tangible results.

   Here's how leadership bridges the gap:

   - Visionary leadership: A compelling vision inspires and rallies the team. Leaders communicate the 'why' behind the strategy, igniting passion and commitment.

   - Strategic decision making: Leaders make tough choices, allocate resources and prioritise initiatives. They navigate uncertainty, balancing short-term imperatives with long-term goals.

- Culture shaping: Leadership influences organisational culture. A culture aligned with strategy fosters innovation, agility and resilience. Effective leaders are not just managers; they are architects of change, orchestrating the execution of strategic intent.

3. **People: the heartbeat of success**

    People are the beating heart of any enterprise. Their collective efforts propel strategy forward:

    - Engaged workforce: Motivated employees drive results. Leaders cultivate engagement by recognising achievements, providing growth opportunities and fostering a sense of purpose.
    - Talent development: Developing skills and competencies ensures that the workforce can execute strategy effectively. Training, mentorship and continuous learning are vital.
    - Collaboration and alignment: Cross-functional collaboration breaks silos. When people understand how their roles contribute to the bigger picture, synergy emerges.

    Remember, people are the carriers of strategy. Their commitment, creativity and adaptability determine success.

So, in conclusion, the relationship between business strategy, leadership and people is symbiotic. A well-crafted strategy without effective leadership and an engaged workforce remains theoretical. Conversely, visionary leadership and motivated people can breathe life into even the most ambitious strategy. When these elements harmonise, organisations thrive, achieving their full potential in the world.

A summary of leadership

So far, we've learnt that leadership is critical in any organisation. Understanding different leadership styles is important to help execute plans and actions for the benefit of the organisation and the team.

Taking the leadership test reaffirms the importance of leaders self-managing, to enable change through their actions, but also to be a good role model in bringing gravitas to their position. Being competent and able to fulfill your role is the basis of the test. If you score well under 50%, then there is work to be done to become an effective leader.

Understanding who the stakeholders are and your impact on them as a leader is just as important as being a leader with a passion for success. You want your communication to be directed and hitting the mark every time. To a degree, leadership is also creative, so sculpting yourself with key leadership traits defines the quality of your leadership within your organisation and your team.

Lastly, leadership can be tough and extreme, and you need the courage to navigate the finer elements of it. Managing VUCA (Volatility, Uncertainty, Complexity, Adversity) and developing a learning culture puts you in the frame of action to take on any modern-day challenge. To close off this chapter, let's have a look at two well-known leaders that everyone can associate great leadership with.

Jacinda Ardern, former Prime Minister of New Zealand, exemplified a unique and effective leadership style. Ardern's leadership was rooted in kindness. She believed that leaders should prioritise empathy and care for others, rather than focusing solely on power. During the pandemic, Ardern communicated openly with her nation through live Facebook chats and Q&A sessions. Her relatable approach helped people understand the situation and adhere to lockdown restrictions. Ardern emphasised empathy as a crucial quality for leaders. She blended strength with understanding, making decisions that considered the circumstances of others and future generations.

Ardern consistently made decisions based on a clear set of values. Her humility and relatability helped inspire trust among those she led. Rejecting traditional gender norms, Ardern communicated decisions with morals and empathy. She fostered trust and collaboration, creating a culture of purpose and shared vision.

In summary, Ardern's leadership style combined kindness, empathy and authenticity, making her a role model for leaders worldwide.

John Winston Howard, former Prime Minister of Australia, exhibited a multifaceted leadership style during his extensive political career spanning four decades (from the 1970s to 2007). Key aspects of his leadership centred, to a degree, on his combative approach. He engaged in robust debates and was unafraid to take a firm position on issues. Despite lacking charisma, Howard managed to appeal to voters through transformational leadership. He drew inspiration from challenging life experiences, both in his family upbringing and, later, in politics. His ability to adapt and evolve was remarkable.

Howard oscillated between different leadership styles based on circumstances and his capacity to wield power. At times, he embodied the roles of controller, therapist and messiah. This flexibility allowed him to effectively navigate the political landscape. But it was his narrative and crisis-management skills that helped Howard navigate many global issues on Australian soil. His grasp of storytelling and his awareness of his own limitations enabled his government to win four elections over a decade. During crises, he rose to the occasion, demonstrating resilience and strategic thinking. In summary, Howard's leadership style combined tenacity, adaptability and a keen understanding of the political environment.

In the next chapter, we'll look at the second element of the LIPS framework: Ideas.

3. IDEAS

Within the LIPS framework, ideas are pivotal for several reasons. A courageous and intelligent leader encourages team members to think beyond their immediate surroundings, acknowledging that they don't always hold all the answers. Such leaders actively seek external ideas. There are many ways to do this, but setting the right environment is key. Having an open and transparent approach to problem solving through consultative practices builds a safe and trustworthy workplace for all employees.

Leaders who encourage and champion ideas, recognising that great ideas can come from anyone, regardless of rank or position, foster innovation within their organisations. Adding critical thinking helps leaders structure their thoughts logically, present ideas persuasively and engage in constructive dialogues with their teams. Critical thinking also helps them identify biases, recognise pitfalls and uncover hidden opportunities.

The best way to get to a critical juncture in critical thinking is by asking inspiring questions that stimulate creativity and encourage employees to think beyond the obvious. These questions lead to fresh insights and novel solutions that otherwise may not be considered. Incorporating diverse perspectives is essential for generating innovative ideas. Leaders who value different viewpoints create an environment where creativity thrives.

Through this process, everyone starts to grow closer together because ideas drive collaboration. When leaders facilitate creative collaboration, harnessing new technologies and encouraging cross-functional teamwork, they enhance problem-solving and drive progress.

Ideas are the seeds of innovation and the lifeblood of change and progress within any organisation. They can stem from various sources and be sparked by different processes and environments, but the most common way is when employees, teams and departments generate ideas based on their experiences, expertise and understanding of organisational challenges. Customers, suppliers, competitors and industry trends provide valuable insights and inspiration for new ideas. Interactions between different departments and disciplines can lead to creative solutions that might not emerge within isolated silos. Dedicated research and development (R&D) teams focus on exploring new technologies, processes and products every day.

So by now, you may be thinking, 'it's well and good that we know what leaders should be doing, but how should leaders help generate ideas within their organisations and teams?' There are five tried-and-tested methods that work and can be executed by anyone if the intention is to garner team engagement and results from the exercises.

Five tried-and-tested exercises

Exercise 1: Brainstorming sessions. Facilitated meetings where participants are encouraged to freely share and discuss ideas without judgement or criticism. Notepads, whiteboards and sticky notes, to name a few, are some tools that can get anonymous ideas out into the open, giving team members ownership and responsibility in the process.

Exercise 2: Mind mapping. This is a visual tool that helps with organising and structuring ideas, showing relationships and hierarchies between different concepts. Getting a team around a whiteboard with markers and a free rule to build on every thought, interconnecting each with the other, is a great way to build a sense of common purpose.

Exercise 3: SWOT analysis. This involves identifying **S**trengths, **W**eaknesses, **O**pportunities and **T**hreats to generate strategic ideas that capitalise on strengths and opportunities while addressing weaknesses and threats. No answer is wrong and the bigger the list the more comprehensive detail you have.

Exercise 4: SCAMPER method. This method is a creative thinking technique that stands for **S**ubstitute, **C**ombine, **A**dapt, **M**odify, **P**ut to another use, **E**liminate and Reverse. It helps participants to think about a problem or opportunity in different ways.

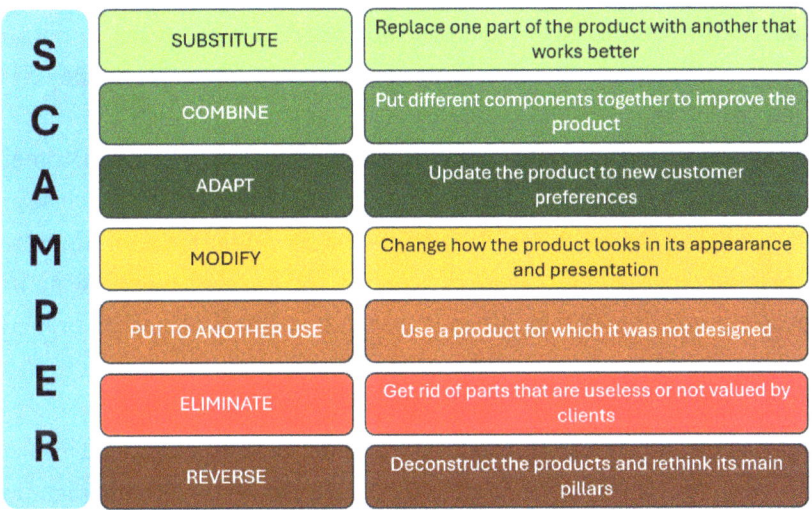

Exercise 5: Crowdsourcing. This involves engaging a large group of people, either within or outside the organisation, to gather a diverse range of ideas. Conferences and management retreats in a different atmosphere are a perfect way to maximise this methodology.

Ideas = the seeds of innovation

Ideas are the foundation of innovation. They stem from creative thinking and are essential for solving problems and improving processes. Effective leaders cultivate a culture where ideas are encouraged and valued.

The journey from idea generation to implementation involves several stages –evaluation, development and execution – as we have already discovered. Leadership plays a critical role in facilitating this process by providing the necessary resources and support. The only barriers to innovation include organisational inertia, lack of resources and resistance to change.

Leaders must identify and mitigate these barriers quickly to foster an innovative culture. I can comfortably say that great leadership directly influences the generation and implementation of ideas in any organisation. Transformational leaders, for instance, create an environment that encourages creative thinking and innovation from the minute an employee steps into his office, table or workstation, to the time they clock off to go home.

Leaders who have a solid understanding of their culture barometer appreciate that if the best ideas come from their people, then a diverse and engaged workforce is more likely to generate a wider range of innovative ideas, stay engaged and be more active in the business, overflowing into greater retention of key people and the security of their intellectual property.

Developing the seeds

Once ideas are generated, they need to be refined and developed into viable solutions. This process involves evaluation, prototyping and planning. One method is a value–ease matrix exercise that allows you to plot your ideas down on a two-by-two table (2 x 2). You can only do this when you have developed 'rules' of engagement. This is the evaluation criteria you need to organise and structure your ideas. It by no means takes away your creativity, it just augments your ability to fully explore your concepts. The other considerations are scale, ability to develop quickly and planning.

Here are some dedicated criteria to consider for this part of the ideation process.

> **A. Feasibility.** Assessing whether the idea is practical and can be implemented with the available resources.
>
> **B. Impact.** Determining the potential benefits and value the idea can bring to the organisation and its stakeholders.

C. **Alignment**. Ensuring that the idea aligns with the organisation's vision, mission and strategic goals.

D. **Market potential**. Evaluating the market demand and potential profitability of the idea.

E. **Prototyping and experimentation**. Creating quick and inexpensive models of the idea to test its feasibility and functionality.

F. **Pilot programs**. Implementing the idea on a small scale to evaluate its performance and gather feedback before full-scale deployment.

G. **Iterative development**. Continuously refining the idea based on feedback and testing results, following a cycle of development, testing and improvement.

H. **Resource allocation**. Identifying the resources needed to develop and implement the idea, including time, budget and personnel.

I. **Timeline**. Establishing a timeline for the development and implementation phases, with clear milestones and deadlines.

J. **Risk assessment**. Identifying potential risks and developing mitigation strategies to address them.

Implementing ideas into action

Now the ideas have been through a rigorous and robust process, turning developed ideas into reality involves a structured approach to ensure successful execution and integration into the organisation's operations. These approaches include developing a detailed project plan that outlines the tasks, responsibilities, timelines and resources required for implementation and ensuring that all stakeholders are informed about the idea, its benefits and the implementation plan.

Clear communication helps to gain support and reducing resistance. Providing necessary training and support to employees who will be involved in or affected by the implementation is essential to ensure they have the skills and knowledge needed to succeed. It's also vital to continuously monitor the implementation process to ensure it stays on track. Regular evaluations help in identifying and addressing any issues promptly.

Changing management in the ideation realm

Implementing new ideas often involves change, which can be met by resistance. Effective change management strategies are essential for smooth implementation. Strong support from leadership can drive the acceptance and success of new ideas. Leaders should actively champion the idea and provide the necessary resources and support. Engaging stakeholders early in the process and involving them in decision making helps to gain their buy-ins and support. Transparent and frequent communication about the changes, their benefits and how they will be implemented reduces uncertainty and builds trust, and providing training to help employees develop the skills and knowledge needed to adapt to the changes ensures a smoother transition. Establishing channels for feedback allows employees to express concerns and suggestions, which can be addressed to improve the implementation process.

Despite the best efforts, several barriers can hinder the generation, development and implementation of ideas. Identifying and addressing these barriers is crucial for fostering a culture of innovation. Things like a resistance to change and a preference for maintaining the status quo can stifle innovation, while insufficient time, budget and personnel can prevent ideas from being fully developed and implemented. A fear of failure and the potential risks associated with new ideas can discourage employees from proposing and pursuing innovative solutions. Lack of clear communication about the value and benefits of new ideas can lead to misunderstandings and resistance – and my pet hate, silo mentality – where departments work in isolation rather than collaborating – can limit the sharing and development of ideas.

The positive news is that we have identified what can stop us from growing, which means we can act and put in place various activities to make sure we don't get cut down, such as fostering a culture of innovation by encouraging creativity, experimentation and risk-taking by recognising and rewarding innovative efforts. Allocating adequate time, budget and personnel to support the development and implementation of new ideas can be an inexpensive exercise if you have truly done your homework. One of my favourite activities is promoting cross-functional collaboration and the sharing of ideas across departments. Don't forget to develop strategies to manage and mitigate the risks associated with new ideas, reducing fear and uncertainty.

Leaders should actively support and champion innovation, creating an environment where new ideas are welcomed and valued.

The role of technology
Technology plays a significant role in facilitating the generation, development and implementation of ideas. Various tools and platforms can enhance creativity, collaboration and efficiency. Leveraging data analytics to evaluate the feasibility and potential impact of ideas will provide insights for informed decision making.

Technology has accelerated with the advent of AI, and there are many platforms that allow employees to submit and share ideas easily, ensuring that valuable insights are not lost. Project management tools have never been in greater demand in helping to plan, organise and manage the implementation of ideas, ensuring that projects stay on track. AI can help to analyse large volumes of data to identify trends, patterns and opportunities for innovation. Blockchain technology can enhance transparency and trust in collaborative innovation efforts, particularly in decentralised environments. The Internet of Things (IoT) can provide real-time data and insights that inspire new ideas for improving processes, products and services.

Ideas are the foundation of innovation and play a critical role in driving organisational success. By fostering a culture that encourages creativity and collaboration, providing the necessary resources and support, and effectively managing the development and implementation of ideas, organisations can harness the power of innovation to achieve their strategic goals.

Overcoming barriers to innovation and leveraging technology to facilitate idea management are essential for creating an environment where new ideas can thrive. Understanding the inter-relationship between ideas, leadership, people, and strategy provides a comprehensive framework for fostering innovation and achieving sustained success.

A summary of ideas strategy

Fostering a culture of ideas in a business involves creating an environment where employees feel encouraged, supported and rewarded for their creativity and innovation. There are several strategies businesses can implement to achieve this:

1. **Leadership commitment where leaders lead by example**

    Leaders should actively participate in idea generation and be open to new suggestions. Demonstrating a commitment to innovation from the top sets the tone for the entire organisation.

2. **Open communication**

    Leaders encourage transparent communication where employees at all levels can share ideas without fear of negative repercussions.

3. **Encouraging collaboration**

    Leaders create cross-functional teams, forming diverse teams with members from different departments to encourage a variety of perspectives and ideas.

4. **Collaborative tools**

    Leaders and teams implement collaboration tools and platforms that make it easy for employees to share and develop ideas collectively.

5. **Creating a safe environment**

   Leaders fostering an atmosphere where employees feel safe to take risks and share their thoughts without fear of criticism or failure.

6. **Leaders measuring, encouraging, refining, trying – and failing**

   A learning process where failure is seen as an opportunity to learn and improve, rather than as a setback. The process also measures the impact of implemented ideas on business outcomes to understand what works and what doesn't, where a state of continuously refining idea generation processes based on feedback and results delivers greater success factors in the future.

7. **Providing resources and time**

   Dedicated time is allocated for employees to work on new ideas or side projects – like Google's 20% time. Leaders ensure employees have access to the necessary resources, including technology, training and materials to develop their ideas.

8. **Recognition and rewards**

   Offering incentives for innovative ideas, such as bonuses, promotions or public recognition. Organising idea contests or innovation challenges with rewards for the best suggestions.

9. **Continuous learning and development**

   Offering training programs focused on creative thinking, problem-solving and innovation techniques. Encouraging continuous learning by supporting attendance at conferences, workshops, and other educational events.

10. **Customer and market focus**

    Regularly gathering and integrating customer feedback to inspire new ideas that address real needs and market demands. Staying informed about market trends and emerging technologies to inspire forward-thinking ideas.

11. **Physical and virtual environment**

    Providing creative spaces. Design physical spaces that encourage creativity, such as open-plan offices, breakout areas and brainstorming rooms. For remote teams, provide virtual environments that facilitate idea sharing and collaboration.

By implementing these strategies, businesses can create a vibrant culture where ideas flourish, leading to sustained innovation and competitive advantage.

Inspirational ideas people

Here are some examples of innovative thinkers and ideas implementers whose companies have thrived as they recreated and redeveloped their value propositions through ideation.

<u>Elon Musk – The ideas man</u>

One prominent 'ideas person' in modern-day business is Elon Musk. He is renowned for his visionary approach and his ability to turn ambitious ideas into reality across various industries.

He has founded and led multiple groundbreaking companies, including:

- **Tesla:** Revolutionising the automotive industry with electric vehicles and advancing renewable energy solutions.
- **SpaceX:** Pioneering private space exploration with goals such as reducing space transportation costs and eventually enabling human colonisation of Mars.
- **Neuralink:** Developing brain–machine interface technology to enhance human cognitive abilities and treat neurological conditions.

- **The Boring Company:** Aiming to reduce traffic congestion through innovative tunnelling and infrastructure projects.
- **SolarCity:** Promoting solar power and sustainable energy solutions.

Musk is known for his bold visions, setting audacious goals (such as creating a self-sustaining colony on Mars), developing a high-speed transportation system (Hyperloop) and achieving full vehicle autonomy with Tesla's self-driving technology. His work spans multiple fields, including automotive, aerospace, energy and artificial intelligence, showcasing his ability to integrate and apply ideas across diverse domains.

Where his impact has been felt most, however, is in industry trends, where Musk's ideas have significantly influenced industry and spurred competition and innovation among other companies. His emphasis on sustainability and renewable energy has had a lasting impact on the automotive and energy sectors.

Musk is also known for taking significant risks and persevering through challenges. His companies have faced numerous obstacles, yet he remains committed to his vision, often investing his own money to keep projects afloat. He effectively uses social media and public appearances to share his ideas, generate excitement and rally support from both investors and the public. His communication style helps to build a strong following and drive the momentum needed for his projects.

Musk's combination of innovative thinking, ambitious vision, and ability to execute complex ideas makes him a standout figure in modern business as a great ideas person.

Jeff Bezos – Amazon

Jeff Bezos transformed Amazon from an online bookstore into a global e-commerce and technology giant. His focus on customer obsession, innovation and long-term thinking has led Amazon to dominate online retail, cloud computing (AWS) and various other sectors.

His notable achievements have been pioneering and popularising online shopping and 1-click purchasing, developing and establishing Amazon Web Services (AWS) as the leading cloud services provider, and expanding into diverse areas such as artificial intelligence, logistics, space travel and entertainment.

Satya Nadella – Microsoft

Since becoming CEO in 2014, Satya Nadella has led Microsoft through a significant transformation, focusing on cloud computing, AI and enterprise services. His leadership has revitalised the company's culture and strategic direction. His achievements include leading the shift to cloud computing with Azure, making Microsoft a leader in the space; acquiring LinkedIn, GitHub and other strategic assets to strengthen Microsoft's ecosystem; and promoting a growth mindset culture within Microsoft, leading to increased innovation and collaboration.

Tim Cook – Apple

With big shoes to fill following on from Steve Jobs, Tim Cook has successfully maintained Apple's innovative edge while significantly expanding its market reach. He has focused on sustainability, privacy and expanding Apple's product and service offerings. Like Steve Jobs, Tim Cook has overseen the launch of successful products like the Apple Watch and Air Pods; expanded Apple's services segment with Apple Music, Apple TV+ and Apple Pay, creating greater wealth for shareholders; and maintained Apple's leadership position in the marketplace. Committing to environmental initiatives by aiming for a net-zero carbon footprint has given Apple more credibility with a broader base of consumers.

Reed Hastings – Netflix

Reed Hastings transformed Netflix from a DVD rental service into a global streaming powerhouse. His vision and execution in digital streaming and content creation have revolutionised the entertainment industry. Transitioning Netflix to a streaming service, pioneering subscription-based content consumption, Hastings has shown what a focus on the customer and consumption can do. Investing heavily in original content, leading to critically acclaimed shows and movies, Hastings has expanded Netflix's global presence, reaching audiences in over 190 countries.

Sheryl Sandberg – Meta

As COO, Sheryl Sandberg has played a crucial role in Facebook's growth and development, particularly in monetisation strategies and operational efficiency. Her work has significantly influenced the digital advertising landscape. By developing Facebook's advertising platform, Sandberg has turned it into a major revenue source. Meanwhile she has also been promoting initiatives for women in leadership and gender equality through her book *Lean In* and the Lean In foundation. Sandberg has not only stamped her authority in the global IT landscape but steered Facebook through various challenges and scaled its operations globally.

Mary Barra – General Motors (GM)

As CEO, Mary Barra has been leading GM's transformation towards electric vehicles and autonomous driving. She has focused on innovation, sustainability and repositioning GM as a future-forward company. Being able to take one of the oldest car manufacturers and commit it to an all-electric future says volumes about her ability to drive great ideas and develop them into business strategies. Investing in autonomous vehicle technology and partnerships to advance self-driving cars, Barra has also prided herself in promoting a culture of safety, quality and continuous improvement within GM.

These leaders exemplify how visionary ideas, strategic thinking and effective leadership can drive substantial transformation in their respective industries. To explore this a little further, let us look at their specific leadership styles and how these have contributed to their success:

- **Elon Musk:** Leadership Style – Visionary and transformational
  Characteristics: Bold vision, hands-on, risk-taker, inspirational

- **Jeff Bezos:** Leadership Style – Customer-centric and innovative

  Characteristics: Customer obsession, long-term thinking, operational excellence, data-driven

- **Satya Nadella:** Leadership Style – Transformational and empathetic

  Characteristics: Growth mindset, empathy, strategic vision, collaborative

- **Tim Cook:** Leadership Style – Operational and strategic

  Characteristics: Operational efficiency, steady leadership, client-driven, ethical

- **Reed Hastings:** Leadership Style – Disruptive and innovative

  Characteristics: Innovative thinking, adaptability, empowerment, data-driven

- **Sheryl Sandberg:** Leadership Style – Operational and inspirational

  Characteristics: Operational excellence, inspirational, strategic planning, communication

- **Mary Barra:** Leadership Style – Transformational and inclusive

  Characteristics: Transformational vision, inclusivity, safety and quality focused, resilience

These leaders demonstrate a variety of effective leadership styles, each tailored to their unique business contexts and challenges. But the biggest challenge they faced every year was what was next, and where would the next 'big thing' come from. By adopting all the leadership qualities that have been discussed, they and their companies have flourished in a challenging world order.

4. PEOPLE

The critical role of people in organisations

In today's dynamic business environment, the success of an organisation increasingly depends on its most valuable asset – its people. In the LIPS framework, people play an indispensable role in various aspects of the success of a business, including talent management, employee engagement and team dynamics. Employees are not merely components of the corporate structure. Individuals are the core of any organisation, the driving force behind innovation, productivity and growth. Viewing the importance of people through the lenses of leadership and idea generation highlights their essential contribution to the organisation's success.

If people are the core of a successful organisation, then leadership is the foundation. Effective leaders go beyond mere management; they inspire, motivate and create a culture of excellence. A leader's capacity to engage with employees, understand their needs and promote a collaborative environment is crucial for achieving organisational success.

Leaders provide a clear vision and direction, ensuring that all team members understand the organisation's goals and their role in achieving them. This sense of purpose drives employees to contribute their best efforts, aligning individual performance with organisational objectives.

Good leaders are adept at motivating their teams. They recognise and reward achievements, provide constructive feedback and support professional growth. This not only boosts morale but also enhances job satisfaction and retention rates. A motivated workforce is more likely to be innovative and committed to the organisation's success.

As business management author Patrick Lencioni says, trust is a crucial element in any relationship, especially between leaders and their teams. Leaders who demonstrate integrity, transparency and empathy foster a trusting environment where employees feel safe to express their ideas and take risks. This trust is the bedrock of effective collaboration and collective problem-solving.

Effective leaders identify and nurture potential leaders within their organisations. By mentoring and providing growth opportunities, they ensure a pipeline of capable leaders ready to take on future challenges. This succession planning is vital for the long-term sustainability and growth of the business.

Ideas and innovation are the lifeblood of any organisation seeking to thrive in a competitive market. The ability to generate, refine and implement new ideas is crucial for continuous improvement and growth. Employees, because they are at the forefront of operations, are in a unique position to contribute valuable insights and creative solutions.

Organisations that value diversity and inclusion benefit from a wide array of perspectives and ideas. Employees from different backgrounds bring unique viewpoints that can lead to innovative solutions. Encouraging diversity in thought and experience fosters a creative environment where new ideas can flourish.

Employees who are empowered to share their ideas and participate in decision-making processes are more likely to identify problems and propose effective solutions. This proactive approach to problem-solving enhances operational efficiency and drives continuous improvement, which is essential for maintaining a competitive edge. When employees feel that their ideas are valued and have a real impact on the organisation, their engagement and sense of ownership increase. This intrinsic motivation leads to higher productivity, improved quality of work and a stronger commitment to the organisation's goals.

In the digital age, the integration of technology and innovation is paramount. Employees who are tech-savvy and forward-thinking can drive digital transformation initiatives, optimising processes and creating new business models. This adaptability is crucial for organisations to stay relevant and capitalise on emerging opportunities.

Empathy is an important quality for any team manager. Leaders with high emotional intelligence understand and manage not only their own emotions but also those of their team members. Empathy allows leaders to connect with employees on a personal level, fostering a supportive and nurturing work environment. This emotional connection is essential for building strong, resilient teams.

The business landscape is constantly evolving, and organisations must be adaptable to survive and thrive. Employees who are resilient and adaptable are better equipped to handle change and uncertainty. Leaders who cultivate these qualities within their teams ensure that the organisation can navigate challenges and seize new opportunities.

Continuous learning and development are crucial for personal and professional growth. Organisations that invest in the development of their people foster a culture of excellence and innovation. By providing opportunities for learning and skill enhancement, leaders ensure that their teams remain competitive and capable of driving growth.

Ethical leadership and a commitment to corporate social responsibility are also increasingly important in today's business world. Leaders who prioritise ethical behaviour and social impact inspire trust and loyalty among employees and stakeholders. This ethical foundation enhances the organisation's reputation and contributes to sustainable growth.

To sum up, through effective leadership, employees are empowered, motivated and engaged. They become active contributors to the organisation's vision and goals. The generation and implementation of innovative ideas are critical for growth, and it is the people within the organisation who drive this creative process. By fostering a culture of trust, collaboration and continuous improvement, leaders ensure that their organisations are not only competitive but also resilient and adaptable in the face of change. The symbiotic relationship between leadership and ideas generation underscores the undeniable importance of people in achieving organisational success.

Coaching for effective leadership

Helping people find their true purpose

Coaching is something I have done throughout my professional career – and continue to do. It has shaped my leadership style, the way I approach work and how results are delivered. I have mentored individuals through work experiences and sport and have helped many people either come into organisations, grow in organisations or develop themselves to find their true 'ikigai' – their purpose. Of these success stories, some were planned and organised, while others – perhaps the best – have been organic. And a word to the wise: while you may think you will receive gushing gratitude from those you help, this seldom happens. Of course, there are some who are appreciative of your assistance and take the time to return the favour, but if you set out for compliments and stardom through the coaching process, you will be truly disappointed.

My personal joy has always come from seeing people grow in their roles and become something they hoped for – in many instances this happens in spite of their best endeavours to resist through fear of the unknown. At times, I have deliberately pushed the envelope to move an individual to a different place – a better place – whether they realised it or not, and I can still hear them murmuring my name in frustration. Nevertheless, most are now in a role they prefer and operate better in or have substantially grown from where they started. It is truly satisfying to know they are living their best professional careers.

From an employee perspective, if you want someone to coach you, mentor you and guide you through your next steps, choose carefully! You want someone who has scars, been in the wars; experienced the highs and lows of the work environment; come up against good and bad boards, board members and chairpersons; and despite all that have a positive expectancy of the future and are successful – because they will truly challenge you to reflect on your worst self to get your best self, turning up every day in the future. Choose experience over razzle-dazzle any day.

If you are:

- regularly giving friends or peers advice;
- listening to others' problems and offering help and support;
- explaining to people how to do something better;
- giving other people feedback on their behaviours so they can improve…

… then you are already coaching in its rawest form.

Planned or not. The great thing about experienced coaches is that they have myriad techniques that can help you unlock secrets about yourself. I liken it to being in a blacked-out room searching for a way out, finding the key on the floor, searching for the keyhole next, finding it and then finding the door and opening it to a new, enriched light. Sounds dramatic, but I am illustrating the diligence you need to exercise to conquer the barriers that stunt personal growth.

<u>Developing success from failure</u>

Failure can be a stepping stone to success if we approach it with the right mindset and strategies. Good coaches and thoughtful leaders will have plenty of tips to help you turn your failures into opportunities for growth and achievement.

Rather than viewing failure as a setback, consider it a valuable tool for learning. Analyse what went wrong, identify areas for improvement and adjust your approach accordingly. This can be done through a self-assessment audit – a candid one! Here are some tips:

- **Try separate 'failing' from 'failure'.** Understand that failing at a specific task or goal doesn't define you as a failure. It's a temporary setback, not a permanent label. Separate the action (failing) from your overall identity (failure).
- **A good coach will help you define what success means to you.** Success varies from person to person, so reflect on your

own definition of success, whether it's financial stability, personal growth or achieving specific goals. Align your efforts with your personal vision of success. Write down your goals and aspirations.

- **Keep it professional.** I have learnt this the hard way. When facing failure, maintain professionalism. Avoid blaming others or dwelling on negative emotions. Instead, focus on constructive solutions and professional growth through either re-learning skills or working with your coach to map out next steps. Reflection and time out can help bring you back from the brink.

- **To grow, you must take responsibility.** I have seen many professionals abdicate their responsibility in their roles. Instead, acknowledge your role in the failure. Taking responsibility allows you to learn from mistakes and make the necessary adjustments – but, more importantly, build an authenticity that can't be faked, and which people will respect.

- **Have confidence and stay committed.** Believe in your abilities and stay committed to your goals. Confidence helps you bounce back from setbacks and continue working towards success. This can also be called resilience.

- **They say the best form of defence is offence – so move forward rather than dwelling on mistakes.** Dwelling on past mistakes can hinder progress – and worrying what people think will kill you. I recall one person destroying my character to recruiters to make themselves feel better, making themselves out to be the victim to gain sympathy and notoriety. I could have sunk even lower, but I chose to use the lessons learned from their negativity to propel myself towards future achievements. So should you!

- **Lastly, remember, stepping back and taking a break can provide clarity.** Take some time to re-evaluate your goals, adjust your strategies and set new targets based on what you've learned.

Remember, failure is not the end – it's an opportunity to learn, grow and, ultimately, achieve greater success. Your coach will help you through it.

Resolving work-related anxiety

The key to dealing with anxiety and day-to-day pressures is to reframe and counteract each one individually

	Anxiety areas all people struggle with	How to resolve the anxiety
1	Fear of criticism and rejection	Lead and show open communication and allow vulnerability
2	Need for constant reassurance in your role	Work on trust and building up your self esteem
3	Being timid amongst peers and lacking confidence	Assertiveness education and making the first move
4	Overbearing and oversharing	Share of self in increments and small steps with familiarity
5	Losing yourself in relationships and work	Find and commit to values as well as follow a passion
6	Intolerance of partner availability	Build up passions, hobbies and interests for yourself
7	Jealous and insecure	Practice open communication and being vulnerable
8	Prioritising others over yourself	Self-worth work and therapy to build control and balance
9	Overanalysing and worrying	Practice mindfulness, meditating and journaling topics
10	Dependency and co-dependency	Independence and interdependence
11	Intolerance of being alone and isolated	Try solo projects first and practice developing friendships
12	Moodiness, impulsiveness and being unstable	Practice mindfulness and meditation
13	Being clingy and needy all the time	Develop independence and have self-worth

EASY TO SUGGEST BUT TAKES DISCIPLINE, TRUST AND FAITH TO MAKE THE CHANGES. IT WILL CHANGE IF YOU WANT IT TO

Work anxiety can be challenging, but there are several strategies a coach can use to help manage it effectively. Here are some I have used with people to help them overcome work-related anxiety.

- **A great coach will question your thought patterns.** Sounds confronting, but they will ask you to discuss the unhelpful negative thoughts that can take root in your mind and distort the severity of a situation. They will challenge your fears by asking if they're true and by helping you to consider where you can regain control.

- **Exercise can help.** Regular exercise is a powerful stress reducer and can improve your mood. Low-impact exercises such as walking, yoga and tai chi can reduce stress and manage anxiety symptoms. It's a good idea to incorporate exercise into professional meetings – instead of meeting in the office, walking outdoors and discussing topics at the same time can get stuff done in a low-stress way. Focused deep breathing exercises can also be hugely beneficial. Sitting by yourself or with a coach and undertaking measured breathing techniques can help alleviate immediate feelings of anxiety. Try breathing in for four counts then breathing out for four counts for a total of five minutes.

- **The '333 rule'.** Being self-aware, and in tune with your surroundings, can help you navigate future situations by avoiding stress and anxiety. Try the '333 rule'. Name three things you can see, three sounds you can hear and interact with three things you can touch. This helps you to focus and ground yourself. Writing down anxious thoughts can also help you take stock of your emotions in the moment but, more importantly, help you identify signs of the onset of anxiety.

- **Acknowledge your feelings.** It's essential to admit when you're struggling. Recognise your anxiety and seek ways to cope with it. A call to your coach, to a mentor or loved one is always a good place to start.

- **Practise good time management.** Most anxious moments come from time, or rather a lack of it. Get into routines. Organise your tasks and prioritise them. Having a clear plan can reduce anxiety about deadlines and workload. Exercises like the 'Eisenhower Matrix' can assist in this. Establish limits for work-related tasks. Avoid overcommitting and learn to say no when necessary.
- **Communication is key.** Communicate with your peers, manager, family and friends if you need help or feel overwhelmed. Be vulnerable and discuss things openly with your manager. A great and positive leader will be there to provide support, advice or adjust expectations because they truly care for you and your success.

Remember that everyone experiences anxiety differently, so as a coach you need to find what works best for your team members, clients or mentees.

<u>Visual thinking methodology</u>

Have you ever witnessed an elite athlete at the sidelines of a race or event, eyes closed and almost hypnotically moving from side to side, mimicking the actions they will undergo in their specific event. A particularly graphic example is an aerial skier and a luge competitor who will visualise their jumps, or weave through the turns they will have to make when they take to the field. This is a version of visual thinking or, more precisely, visualisation that coaches encourage their athletes to experience, both to help calm them and also to have them live the race or event before it occurs so they can deliver a seamless performance when it counts.

In executive coaching, a powerful method of communication is visual thinking that allows individuals to express ideas visually, using graphic representation instead of relying solely on verbal descriptions. The key coaching points of visual thinking are organising ideas visually and leveraging images to inspire and recall information. This encourages brainstorming with visual elements, making it easier to express complex concepts and collaborate effectively.

The obvious benefits are where visual thinking helps clarify ideas by creating visual representations that others can easily understand, while stimulating problem-solving and encouraging innovative thinking. This creates an efficiency that teams can improve on by organising ideas graphically and also allows for strong associations between pieces of information.

There are several common visual thinking strategies, such as mind mapping, that connect related concepts or ideas using visual diagrams or storyboarding, sequentially arranging visual elements to tell a story or depict a process.

When dealing with an individual there is a specific eight-step program to follow to build visual thinking superpowers.

1. Define their goal – outline what they want and commit it to paper.
2. Describe the audience the goal is aimed at.
3. Define the actions that need to be modelled. Map out the steps!
4. Define the structure by creating a process of delivery.
5. Synthesise the plan by organising the steps into chunks of actions. Think through the doubters, the bumpers and barriers and how to overcome them.
6. Visualise the answers and note down the positive affirmations!
7. Ensure it will work by reliving every aspect in your mind – test, predict, prove.

Remember, visual thinking isn't limited to artistic individuals; it benefits everyone, especially in professional settings where effective communication and collaboration are crucial. So, go ahead and explore this methodology to enhance your idea-sharing and problem-solving skills.

Team dynamics: forming–storming–norming–performing

FOR GROWTH

FORMING

Feelings: Team members are excited and eager but may also feel some anxiety about fitting in and performing well.

Behaviours: Expect lots of questions from team members as they seek clarity and establish their roles within the team.

Team Tasks: The primary focus is on creating a team structure, defining goals and establishing trust. Task accomplishment may be relatively low during.

STORMING

Feelings: As the team moves toward its goals, members realise that early excitement and expectations can't be fully met.

Behaviours: Teams challenge boundaries, get to know each other better and may experience conflicts.

Team Tasks: Addressing conflicts, clarifying roles and improving communication become essential during this stage.

NORMING

Feelings: Team members start to accept each other's differences and work together more harmoniously.

Behaviours: Normality and group cohesion begin to emerge. Members collaborate effectively.

Team Tasks: Establishing clear norms, improving processes and building stronger relationships are key.

PERFORMING

Feelings: The team is now highly functional, with a shared focus on achieving its goals.

Behaviours: Members work seamlessly together, leveraging their strengths.

Team Tasks: High productivity, effective problem-solving and achieving the team's mission are the main objectives.

TEAM DYNAMICS

In 1965, Bruce Tuckman, an American researcher in group dynamics, proposed the forming–storming–norming–performing model of group development. It is still a tried-and-tested model, and Tuckman, at the time of inception, stated that these phases are necessary for a team to grow, face challenges, tackle problems, find solutions, plan work and deliver results for any organisation, large or small.

Coaching groups of people within an organisation is interesting, to say the least. Obviously, everyone is different, so how do you apply this approach to get the results you desire and a sustainable team?

- Primarily, when it comes to the **Forming** stage, the objective of the coach or leader is to establish a clear team purpose and specific goals. Some of these actions include introducing team members to each other, if they are new, and defining roles and responsibilities. Setting expectations for behaviour and communication frequency is important at this stage. Strategy documents and a cascading strategy approach help smooth understanding of the next steps for everyone.

- **Storming** is all about addressing conflicts and building ongoing trust. This includes actions like encouraging open dialogue and being able to resolve disagreements constructively. The real key to the storming stage is fostering a supportive environment where it is safe and secure for team members to be themselves, as hard as any feedback might be for those involved. This stage requires a level of maturity from all. One-on-one documents, regular quarterly business reviews and feedback loops are a wonderful way to stay on top of this.

- **Norming** is when you get to develop team norms and cohesion through a regular review process, celebrating achievements and progress together. It strengthens collaboration and reinforces trust you have created. Team meetings, town hall exercises and

department catch-ups are a reliable source of feedback loops you can create.
- When these three areas come together, **Performing** is a byproduct of all the challenging work. Achieving high productivity and constructive collaboration where the team feels empowered, continuously improving processes and a focus on results and shared success is the mainstay of this phase of the process. Celebrating team and individual achievement is necessary through recognition programs, and both short-term and long-term incentives are perfect to keep momentum going.

There is a lot of work required, and really adaptability is key here. Keeping records and revisiting successes will ensure you propagate a positive environment for consistent high performance. Regular group meetings, like town hall presentations, help. Even shareholder and yearly conferences are excellent to portray how far you have come as a group.

It's important to note that while Bruce Tuckman's model includes an 'Adjourning' stage, my bias is towards continuous improvement and growth within established businesses, so I have omitted that stage of the model.

For dedicated project teams, staying in place to tackle all required programs and projects within an organisation is key. These teams cycle through small increments of improvements across every aspect of the organisation, for an overall impact. Team members are able and adept, almost like the SAS troops in the military. While the Adjourning stage is critical for acknowledging accomplishments and saying goodbye for small project teams, it's important to remember that teams can develop great interdependencies that can be used for many other internal processes and systems.

So, let's focus on reforming, re-storming, re-norming and outperforming for future projects. As always, it's about delivering ongoing consistent and familiar results.

The Head, Heart and Hands Approach

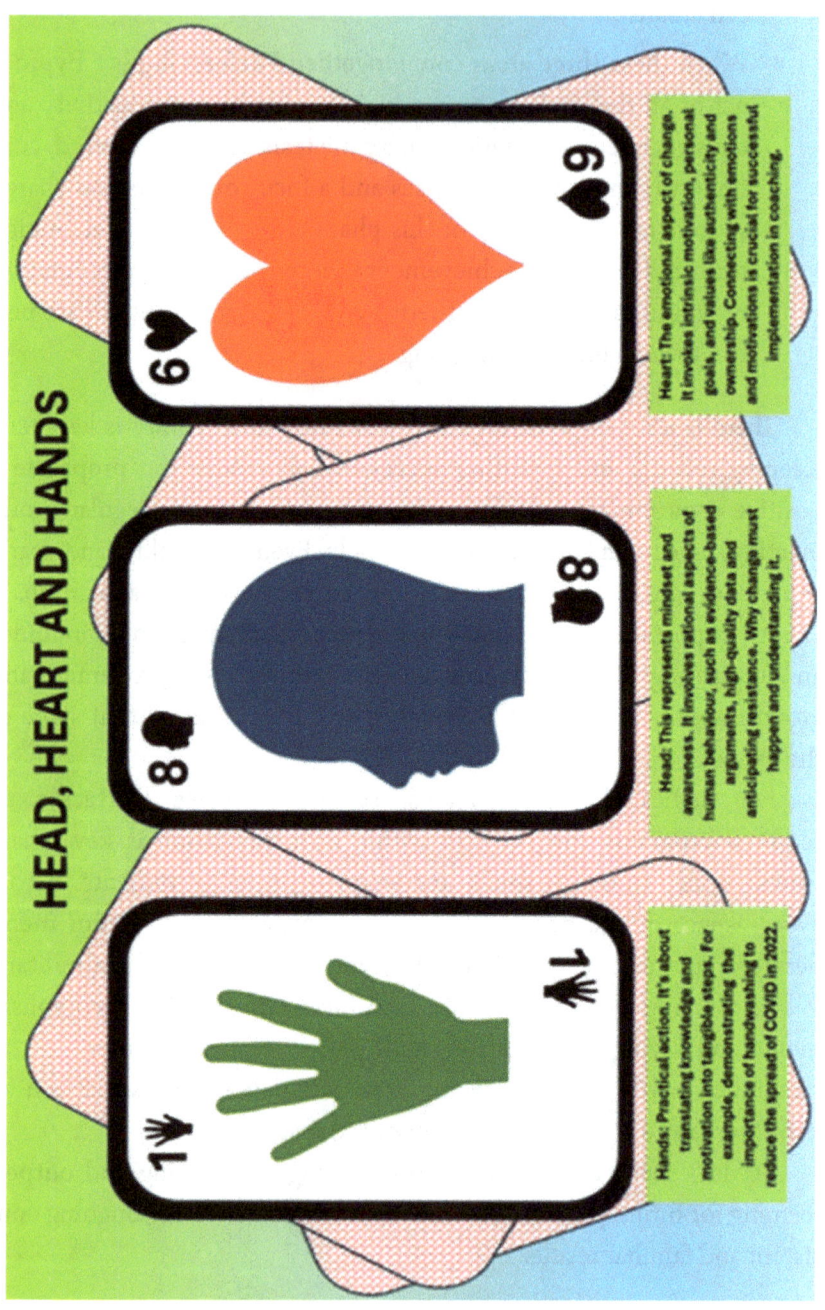

Are you looking for a holistic approach to transformational change and change management? Look no further than the Head, Heart and Hands philosophy. Introduced by educationalist David Orr, this methodology emphasises the interconnecting aspects of rationale, belief and implementation in various contexts, including management and personal development.

In coaching, this means understanding and addressing emotional aspects around motivation and mindset, implementing change effectively and translating practical steps into skill development and execution. It's important to remember that these elements work together, not sequentially, for the delivery of successful transformation.

So, when coaching people, consider all three aspects in parallel, matching your approach to their unique needs and context. By encouraging both the intellectual and emotional aspects while driving authentic actions, you can help create a lasting change in your coachees, mentees and team members.

The Iceberg Principle

Let's delve into the importance of the Head, Heart and Hands concept in coaching teams and change management. Here, the 'Iceberg Principle' provides a valuable lens for understanding team dynamics. Just like an iceberg, where only a small portion is visible above the waterline, team dynamics involve both observable and hidden elements you must be vigilant about.

Above the surface, the observable part of the iceberg is where you see elements such as management's leadership style. You see how the leader's behaviour, communication and decision making influence team morale and productivity. This is the domain of the Hands.

Below the surface, the rest of the iceberg – hidden to the observer – is where hypotheses live. Beneath the waterline lie unspoken beliefs and assumptions. Understanding these emotions is crucial for effective team dynamics. Another is shared values, where deeply ingrained values guide behaviour. This is the domain of both Head and Heart.

So, what advice and application can be suggested to navigate through this safely if you find yourself in an ice flow like the *Titanic* did? Firstly, explore assumptions by encouraging open dialogue. Bring to the surface any assumptions and address any misalignments. To help this process, be sure to acknowledge emotions, creating a safe space for emotional expression.

Addressing hidden assumptions, emotions and values leads to healthier team dynamics and better outcomes. Trust grows when you tackle both visible and hidden aspects.

Remember, just as the *Titanic*'s hidden damage led to its tragic fate, understanding the submerged aspects in your team and organisation, whether in leadership or coaching, can make all the difference to your team dynamic.

Applying the Head, Heart and Hands philosophy

Let's now demonstrate how important this Head, Heart and Hands (H x 3) approach is by exploring a coaching scenario of mine where the Head, Heart and Hands philosophy was successfully applied. The scenario was empowering a new manager. Let's call her Susan.

The background was that Susan, a newly promoted manager, felt overwhelmed by her responsibilities. She lacked confidence in decision making and struggled to connect with her team. She was highly capable but paralysed by anxiety, although you would never have guessed this working with her.

Looking at the Head dimension (Thinking) as her coach, I assessed Susan's knowledge gaps. We discussed her role, the team dynamics and organisational goals. Once comfortable with opening up in her comments, we began to explore different management strategies, problem-solving techniques and decision-making models that we were both comfortable with to move forward.

Moving to the Heart dimension (Feeling), Susan expressed to me the anxiety she felt about her team's expectations. We delved into her fears and motivations, discovering they were totally unfounded but nevertheless critical to unpack. Her emotional awareness was admirable and inspiring. In fact, I shared stories of successful managers who faced similar challenges. We discussed her passion for leadership and her desire to make a positive impact and how important it was to focus on that, as opposed to anything else peripheral to her success.

Then we delved into the Hands dimension (Action). Through action planning we co-created a very simple action plan to tackle some of the hurdles she had mentioned. Susan set specific goals, such as improving communication in meetings, building greater trust and delegating more effectively. To help the approach, we discussed skills and skill development, where we worked on practical skills such as active listening, feedback delivery, conflict resolution and time management.

The result? Susan gained more confidence and clarity. She implemented new strategies, leading to improved team dynamics. Her team members felt more supported and engaged, but more importantly she taught me a few things about getting the best out of coaches.

Remember, successful coaching involves integrating these three elements to create lasting change. It wouldn't have happened, though, if Susan hadn't been willing to open up and be a willing participant. Just as a student arrives when the teacher is ready, learning occurs when both student and teacher are in sync, fostering a conducive environment for growth. H x 3 is all about this. A collaborative approach!

The Head

Knowledge and wisdom are essential components of every leader's thinking. In the 'Head' dimension of the H x 3 model, they sets the foundation for effective decision making and problem-solving when confronted with personal change. Developing a sixth sense, so to speak, where you challenge the mental models and paradigms that have been built up over time, is crucial. Here are some thoughts for you to consider.

When coaching for change in this area, you are helping people improve their self-awareness, as this is essential for personal growth and emotional intelligence. It may sound complicated, but the focus is on the person's thoughts and perspective, as opposed to the person. Over time, people develop thinking that defines their behaviours, and it's this thinking that the Head component really explores.

If you are going through a change process with your coach, you might have questions such as: 'How will this new way of thinking improve my current/thinking situation?' or 'How has my personal mission in business and life been altered and why?' Don't worry, these questions are common.

Here are some practical exercises you can do with a coach or yourself to help you begin the change process in your Head:

- **Strength Assessments:** Take assessments like a Gallup Strengths or Limbic test to understand your core values and strengths. Discuss this with your coach and look to build on the information day by day.
- **Journaling:** Write down your thoughts, emotions and experiences. Regular journaling promotes self-reflection and insight and helps you celebrate the change journey over time.
- **Personal Vision:** Create a new vision statement for your life. Define your purpose, goals and aspirations with your coach and set sail, reviewing it regularly.
- **Observing Others:** Observe how people react in different situations. Learn from their behaviours and consider how it relates to your responses. What can you learn, and what can you avoid?

Remember, self-awareness is a journey, and these exercises can help you develop a deeper understanding of yourself. They can also help you get inside your own Head to master change and allow your coach to work with you in a more sensitive and meaningful way.

The Heart

The Heart is where emotion lives, so it makes sense to get to the heart through storytelling. Storytelling plays a critical role in shifting culture when coaching. When defining culture, stories help define an organisation's history and journey – where it has come from to where it is today. It's the same with people. Your personal stories can sometimes define you as you appear to others.

Narratives shared, whether about past successes, challenges or values, shape team members' and leaders' understanding of what's valued or shunned. They help to reinforce change because storytelling ensures that key messages resonate. Meaningful stories transform opinions, attitudes and behaviours, leading to more inspirational buy-in for change.

When leaders and coaches share personal experiences or illustrate cultural shifts through narratives with team members and clients, it builds trust and encourages alignment with the desired culture. This is one of the quickest ways to get the ball rolling in change management and personal success.

Through storytelling you can bring things to light that help to expunge often suppressed feelings and sensations that are stifling personal development and growth. A good story with meaning can be uplifting and help coaches navigate to the heart of the matter with clients, coachees and mentees.

This is where you earn your reputation as a coach. Getting to the Heart is a very important element to get right.

The Hands

Now I want to concentrate on the final element – the Hands. The Hands dimension constitutes the demonstrable actions that most specifically indicate that change is happening and whether your coaching is having the desired result for both you and your coachee/client/mentee. For a coach, the Hands element is all about looking for specific behaviours – different behaviours – and comments/actions you have never noticed before. Most of these behaviours would have been shaped or moulded through the conversations you have had together regarding elements of development and change.

The most important questions most coaches ask themselves are: 'What am I seeing differently, and does it line up with what the client/

coachee/mentee wants in the long run?', 'What have they stopped, started and continued doing that demonstrates change?' and 'Are they performing their job differently?'

Most interestingly, the coachee/client/mentee would be saying the same to themselves, and if there is self-doubt and uncertainty about the future, as change can be confronting, they may be also asking themselves: 'What am I supposed to be doing differently from yesterday?'

This is where, as a coach, you need to be in the moment and walk them through what the result will look like while staying on track and practising the actions you have planned to take together.

As a coach, you must balance the devices and tools I have talked about with one-on-one teaching – especially coaching and realigning your client/coachee/mentee back to the desired state – and, lastly, taking on the feedback and challenges posed. This is a key point in your relationship where strength of character, resilience and deep trust are generated, because through recognising the smallest wins and celebrating change, you are pushing and guiding your coachee/mentee/client forward.

I have found a simple 'stop, start, continue' exercise really gets the ball rolling in these conversations and, combined with regular one-on-one help, gets to the crux of change and movement forward.

Putting it all together: H x 3 methodology in coaching and modern leadership

In the ever-evolving landscape of leadership and coaching, the H x 3 methodology has emerged as a holistic framework designed to foster comprehensive development in individuals and teams. By integrating cognitive, emotional and practical dimensions, this approach offers a balanced pathway to effective leadership and personal growth.

In practical terms, coaching with the 'Head' involves setting clear goals, understanding the theoretical underpinnings of leadership practices and applying evidence-based strategies.

Coaches encourage leaders to refine their vision, develop robust plans and anticipate challenges through rigorous mental exercises and strategic foresight. In coaching, focusing on the 'Heart' means helping leaders to understand and manage their emotions and those of others.

Coaches work on enhancing interpersonal skills, developing empathy and cultivating a leadership style that is compassionate and people-centric. This approach is crucial in navigating the complexities of human dynamics within teams and organisations, leading to higher morale and better collaboration. In the coaching context, the 'Hands' aspect involves developing practical skills and competencies.

Coaches assist leaders in honing their ability to execute plans, manage projects and lead by example. This hands-on approach ensures that theoretical knowledge and emotional intelligence are effectively integrated into everyday practices, leading to tangible outcomes and sustainable growth.

So, for what it's worth, in my humble opinion, the Head, Heart and Hands methodology offers a comprehensive approach to leadership and coaching, addressing the multifaceted nature of human development. As organisations continue to face unprecedented challenges, VUCA scenarios and opportunities, the H x 3 methodology provides a valuable blueprint for nurturing leaders who can think strategically, feel empathetically and act decisively.

The Johari Window

Now, let's look at team-building models that can enhance collaboration and performance in your business. First up, the Johari Window. This model was developed in 1955 by psychologists Joseph Luft and Harry Ingham to help individuals understand their interpersonal communication and relationships. As a coach, this is a powerful tool for enhancing self-awareness and building trust among individuals or teams.

The Johari Window is a simple 2 x 2 table that features four quadrants: Open Area, Blind Spot, Hidden Area and Unknown Area. Coaches use this methodology to create feedback and self-disclosure between themselves and their clients, but more importantly, in a business setting, it creates two-way teaching between leaders and team members undergoing some form of change and transformation.

By understanding each other, teams can close out knowledge gaps, leading to quicker implementation and delivery of programs. Ideally, through discussion of the different quadrants, this encourages team members to seek feedback from colleagues, friends or family. It also helps them share relevant personal information (without compromising privacy) to reduce the hidden area and foster trust.

Authentic relationships require depth, whereas façades hinder growth, so while team members don't need to reveal embarrassing details, they need to be honest in responding because authenticity builds trust. The Johari Window promotes openness, self-reflection and mutual understanding for personal growth.

Here are five easy steps to follow for a successful team approach:

1. Start with an introduction to the model's four quadrants: Open Area, Blind Spot, Hidden Area and Unknown Area. Emphasise that this exercise aims to enhance mutual understanding and communication.
2. Encourage team members to reflect individually on their own Johari Window. What do they believe is known to others, what might be their blind spots and what is hidden or unknown to them?
3. Pair team members or form small groups for feedback exchange. Share strengths and areas for improvement in a constructive manner.
4. Facilitate a discussion where team members share insights from their feedback exchanges. Discuss common themes, patterns and areas for improvement to understand how self-awareness impacts team dynamics.
5. Use the process to establish team norms and reinforce the importance of trust and vulnerability.

Create a visual representation of the team's collective Johari Window to recall and keep the information for future reference.

Deliver the 5 to Survive!

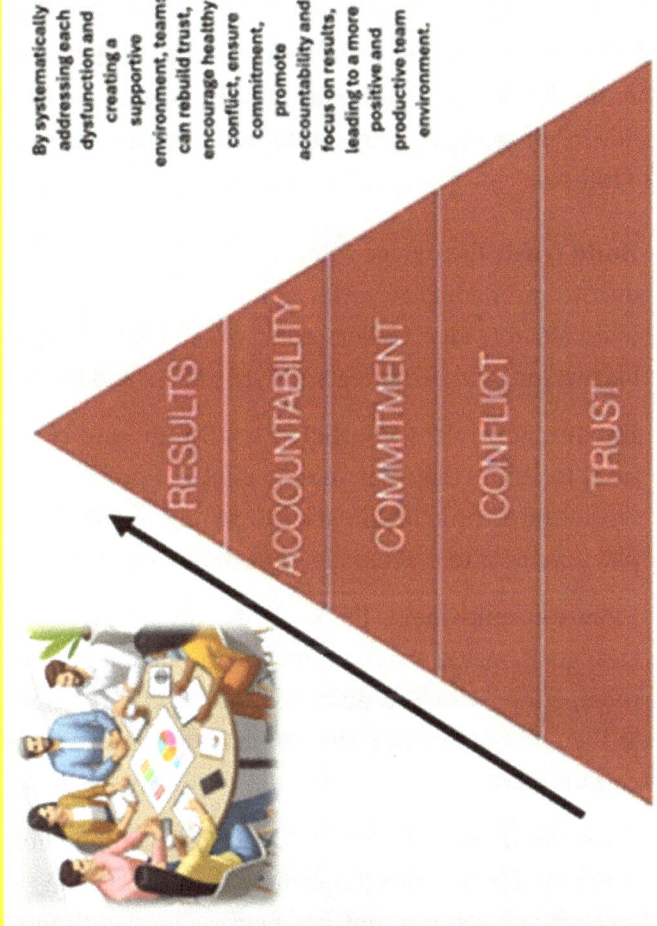

Transforming your team dynamics

Transforming a team that has been lagging can be challenging. However, Patrick Lencioni's book, *The Five Dysfunctions of a Team*, can help you rebuild a more positive team environment. Addressing each of the dysfunctions he describes will transform the team dynamics by fostering a culture of trust, accountability and commitment. Here are the steps to follow:

- **Build trust:** Encourage vulnerability among team members, conduct team-building activities, hold regular one-on-one meetings to understand team members' concerns and strengths, and use tools like personality assessments to help understand each other better.

- **Encourage healthy conflict:** Establish ground rules for discussions to ensure they remain respectful and productive, use conflict resolution techniques like active listening and mediation, and role-play scenarios to practise handling disagreements.

- **Ensure commitment:** Foster clarity and buy-in for decisions, have clear goals, make sure everyone understands their role in achieving them, summarise and document key decisions and action steps at the end of meetings, and set clear deadlines and follow up on commitments.

- **Promote accountability:** Hold each other accountable for performance and behaviours, implement regular check-ins and progress reviews, use metrics and key performance indicators (KPIs) to measure performance, and create a culture where team members feel responsible for both their own and each other's performance.

- **Focus on results:** Keep the team aligned towards common goals, set team goals and celebrate collective achievements, regularly review and communicate progress towards goals, and align individual performance reviews with team objectives to reinforce the importance of team success.

The Change Management Curve

The Change Management Curve model helps us understand the emotional and psychological stages individuals go through during organisational change.

To guide your team through a significant organisational change, the first step is to assess the change's impact and develop a communication plan. It's crucial to ensure that leadership is united and supportive of the change. During the initial stages of shock and denial (Step 1), transparent communication and empathy are essential. Acknowledge feelings of shock and denial and offer support through meetings and open-door policies.

During the stages of anger and resistance (Step 2), provide channels for employees to voice their concerns and frustrations. Take feedback seriously and address valid concerns. Equip employees with the necessary skills and knowledge to handle new systems or processes.

During exploration and acceptance (Step 3), encourage experimentation, celebrate small wins and provide ongoing support and coaching to help team members adapt to new roles or technologies. When fostering commitment and integration (Step 4), empower employees, integrate the new changes into daily routines and organisational culture, and keep the feedback loop open.

To illustrate, let's consider implementing a new project management system. Start with preparation, assessment and a communication plan. When dealing with shock and denial, follow up with detailed emails and FAQs, and offer support. For anger and resistance, organise listening sessions, create a task force and offer training. During exploration and acceptance, start with a pilot program, celebrate wins and offer support. Finally, during commitment and integration, empower teams, reinforce the changes and keep the feedback loop open.

By following these steps, you can guide your team through the emotional and psychological stages of change, ultimately leading to the successful adoption and integration of new initiatives.

KEY ASPECTS OF SELF-ACTUALISATION – EIGHT THAT MAKE YOU GREAT

Realising Potential: It involves recognising and utilising one's talents, abilities and skills to achieve personal goals and ambitions.

Personal Growth: Self-actualisation is about continuous self-improvement and striving to become the best version of oneself.

Authenticity: It requires being true to oneself, embracing one's true nature, and acting in accordance with one's values and beliefs.

Fulfilment and Satisfaction: Ultimately, self-actualisation leads to a deep sense of fulfilment and satisfaction, as individuals feel they are living their life to its fullest potential.

Peak Experiences: Self-actualisation is often associated with peak experiences, which are moments of intense joy, creativity and fulfilment.

Autonomy: It involves a high degree of independence and self-reliance, where individuals take responsibility for their actions and decisions.

Creativity and Innovation: Self-actualised individuals tend to be highly creative and open to new experiences, using their imagination and innovation to solve problems and create value.

Purpose and Meaning: Individuals who are self-actualised often have a strong sense of purpose and meaning in their lives, feeling deeply connected to their work, relationships and personal goals.

Importance of Self-Actualisation

Personal Fulfilment: Achieving self-actualisation leads to a profound sense of personal fulfilment and happiness.

Contribution to Society: Self-actualised individuals often make significant contributions to society, using their talents and skills for the greater good.

Enhanced Relationships: They tend to have healthier and more fulfilling relationships, based on mutual respect and understanding.

Well-Being: Self-actualisation contributes to overall well-being, including mental, emotional and sometimes even physical health.

Characteristics of Self-Actualised Individuals

Self-Awareness: They have a deep understanding of themselves, including their strengths, weaknesses and motivations.

Acceptance: They accept themselves and others without judgement, appreciating human diversity and imperfections.

Problem-Centred: They focus on solving problems that are outside themselves and often work towards causes that benefit others.

Spontaneity: They are spontaneous and natural in their behaviours, not bound by societal expectations or norms.

Empathy and Compassion: They demonstrate a high level of empathy and compassion towards others, often engaging in altruistic activities.

Resilience: They exhibit resilience and the ability to cope with challenges and setbacks effectively.

8-to-be-great Maslow's pointers

In Maslow's hierarchy of needs, self-actualisation is the pinnacle of psychological development. It's about achieving personal growth and realising full potential after basic needs are met. Self-actualised leaders possess unique qualities such as authenticity, purpose-driven emotional intelligence, creativity, autonomy and a thirst for continuous learning. Their focus transcends ego towards collective well-being and inspiring others.

Self-actualisation is a rare state, but when attained, it leads to profound impact. Mentors and coaches play a crucial role in guiding leaders on this journey.

Conflict coaching

Conflict in the workplace is inevitable, but it can be resolved with the help of 'conflict coaching'. This is an effective approach, especially when it comes to addressing conflicts involving leadership. Most issues that arise in the workplace are due to personality clashes between colleagues or team members, leaders managing performance issues with staff, competing priorities, differing opinions impeding team outputs, and rebuilding relationships and trust after an incident has occurred.

What happens when you encounter conflict when coaching an individual or team? It doesn't happen too often, but when you push the boundaries to uncover the real underlying issues of a situation, confrontation can lead to conflict. Here are some examples of conflicts I have seen and helped navigate.

Differing perspectives, where coaches and clients may have opposing viewpoints on goals, strategies or approaches can lead to conflict, and even providing constructive feedback can sometimes trigger disagreements. This is the outcome of an unclear, unplanned approach.

Most scenarios that create these tensions are a byproduct of imagined power dynamics, where the coached/mentee imagines/feels the coach holds too much authority, creating tension. Another scenario may be an ethical dilemma, where the coach is balancing client needs and ethical guidelines. Either way, it's stressful and unproductive and negatively impacts the very reason you are coaching.

To resolve these sorts of situations, take a breath and restart. Announce this intention as you stand up from your chair, or move around from the table, but make a physical change in the space you are sharing with your coachee/mentee and then restart, actively listening to understand one another's viewpoints in the context of the conversation. Another way is to look for common ground between you and then reset boundaries for a refreshed discussion.

Remember, conflict is good and can be an opportunity for growth and learning! Also remember, however, that words can be misunderstood in the heat of the moment, so try to avoid using 'always', 'never', 'you should do' and 'you are'.

Try some of these approaches to diffuse a situation quickly:

1. I can see why you would think that, but this is how I see it.
2. Can I also share my perspective?
3. I think we have different perspectives, but can we find common ground?
4. I'm going to take this evening to reflect on this and get back to you.

Remember, helping means being authentic and sometimes this means the truth, whether we like it or not.

Becoming a Coaching Warrior

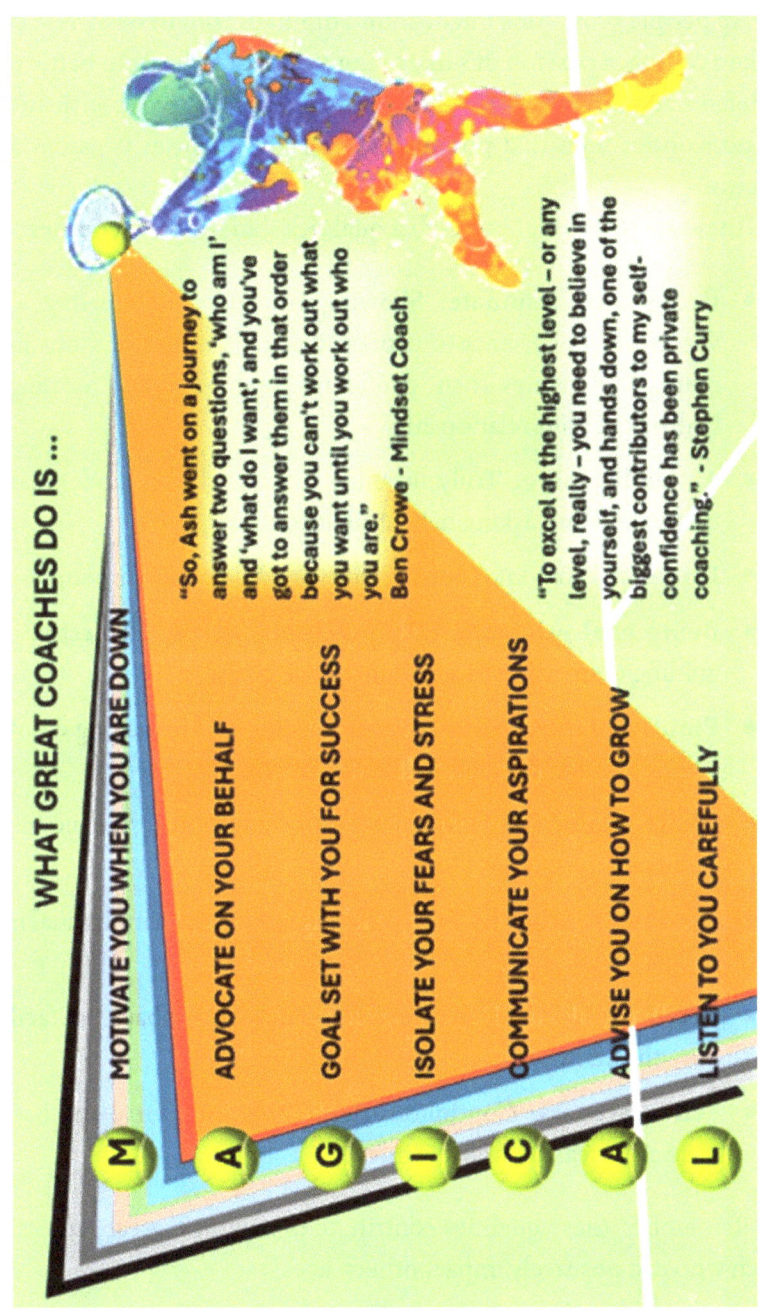

As a professional people coach, you need to harbour an unselfish desire to help people grow. This might sound dramatic, but to be a great coach is like a calling, a passion. It's like being a warrior going into battle ready to defend and advocate on behalf of the people you work with and for. It's no wonder then that possessing the right qualities is essential for success.

These are my thoughts on what qualities shine in great coaches:

- **Being compassionate:** Showing empathy and creating a safe space for your clients to express their challenges without judgement. This creates trust, confidence and reliability, forming the bedrock of your relationship.
- **Active listening:** Truly listening to your clients, understanding their needs and asking insightful questions.
- **Honesty:** Providing candid feedback while remaining supportive.
- **Being goal-oriented:** Helping clients set clear objectives and guiding them towards achieving those goals.
- **Emotional intelligence:** Understanding and managing emotions effectively, both for yourself and your clients.
- **Positive mindset:** Encouraging optimism and resilience in your clients.
- **Flexibility:** Adapting your coaching approach to individual needs and circumstances.
- **Feedback skills:** Delivering constructive feedback to facilitate growth and improvement.
- **Self-awareness:** Continuously reflecting on your own coaching style and areas for improvement.

Remember, these qualities contribute to making a great professional coach who can positively impact others' lives!

One of the best coaching examples I can think of comes from Ash Barty's recent biography where she discusses words that make you a warrior, not a worrier. Her 'Courage Mantra' was the result of her coach working with her to overcome stress before huge tennis matches. He posed critical questions to help her overcome stress and anxiety in her game and have a winning mentality – be a warrior!

Here are a few of them:

1. How do I show up when I am nervous? Silent, violent, flight, fight, freeze, name drop, argue or hope no one asks me a question?

2. When does it happen to me? When I feel judged, when people are staring at me? When I feel like I am losing control of the situation or the match?

3. What can I say to change myself in real time, when it happens next? What can I think that reminds me of strength not weakness? What can I say to myself to make me go tall and not small?

Real gold! Coaching is magical. Practice makes perfect.

People projects

If there is one area of professional life that has both challenged and rewarded me, it's the people I have worked with – their engagement and what they have taught me.

Employee retention is critical to the success and sustainability of every organisation. Companies with high employee turnover risk financial instability and loss of business due to understaffing. Poor morale destroys productivity, and the loss of institutional knowledge can slow a business down to a standstill.

That's why a term I coined – People Projects – is so important to me (and possibly you!). I have had to learn this the hard way. By building retention strategies into your business, you can prioritise and pinpoint your team members' strengths, position them to succeed and grow, and optimise their time to visit, or revisit with other team members who exemplify your vision and mission, especially the company values.

Investing in your people is critical. Each employee should be a mini project within your business. As a leader, stakeholder and/or owner, it's important to think about how your most precious resource fits into the plans for your joint success. By retaining top-performing and highly skilled employees, companies stand a better chance of maintaining or improving productivity, efficiency and innovation.

Remember, customers may perceive a steady stream of new faces as a sign of instability, which can erode brand loyalty and negatively impact sales. By retaining your top talent, you can keep your business strong and growing. Invest in people in the same way as you would business-critical projects, and you'll see your organisation thrive.

Finding the right mentor

Have you been thinking about finding a mentor? It's important to do your due diligence before selecting one. There are many people who are mentors and coaches. It's crucial to find one who has the relevant experience and expertise specific to your field.

TWA: Theorist, Witness and Applicator in mentoring

The Theorist Mentor is academically well-read and qualified; the Witness Mentor has worked directly for successful leaders; and the Applicator Mentor (I also call them the Phoenix) has the most experience and has done it all.

But there's one mentor type, **Trifectas**, that has it all: theory, experience, the ability to overcome hardships, success and connections. They are able to draw on every one of these areas to give the most balanced view. These mentors may be tough in their approach, but they are the best kind to have and are hard to find.

Remember, finding the right mentor is crucial to your success. Do your research, consider their past mentees and professional career, and find the right fit for you.

Seven tips for high-performance coaching

High-performance coaching is a demanding discipline that requires a coach to be a mentor, role model and coach all at once. So, how can you become the best version of a high-performance coach? Here are seven tactics to help you get started:

1. Trademark your approach by defining your vision, values, purpose and strategy with a behavioural blueprint that maps out actions and individual roles and responsibilities.
2. Abandon your ego and be the person who seeds ideas, triggers meaningful conversations and provokes actions and thinking to stay on track.
3. Communicate and provide focused, crystal-clear and continual feedback. Critique behaviours and actions, not personal traits. Recognise and reward good behaviours to accelerate performance.
4. It takes two to tango! Work closely with the team to clarify tasks and develop a clear picture of the needs of the other person.
5. Innovate by leveraging science and the psychology of goal setting and individual KPIs into financial and team objectives, with a time-based measurement.
6. Commit to continuous improvement by developing as a coach at a faster rate than your team. Champion cross-functional collaboration and networks to open thinking and share new perspectives.
7. Storm to perform, where every opportunity is used to help individuals embed learning in a fail-safe environment, performing under pressure, making it a mantra to *practise, practise, practise.*

It takes time to master these tactics, but once you do, you'll never look back. Remember, it's a race against time to get there before others so that you can lead the pack instead of sitting among mediocrity. Start today and see what tomorrow brings.

Seven tips for one-on-one coaching

I can't stress enough the importance of communication in developing a high-performance individual. Whether it's face-to-face communication in teams or one-on-one, there are seven ways you can practice improving your communication skills to bring out the best in someone.

1. **Listen loudly:** Switch off communication devices, suppress your ego and don't give your opinion. Just listen with intent and let the other person shine.
2. **Play catch:** Clarify any uncertain points, paraphrase what is said, ask the speaker to expand and develop a clear picture of their logic.
3. **Look long:** Watch for non-verbal cues to determine intent and whether the other person is procrastinating. Maintain eye contact, open body language and a calm facilitation.
4. **Rightly reflect:** Demonstrate acknowledgement and understanding, and don't superimpose self-held assumptions. Celebrate silence and respond constructively.
5. **Safety first:** Commit to a psychologically safe, open and inclusive environment. Be positive, and accept that failure is an opportunity to learn and encourage interpersonal risk-taking.
6. **Take turns:** Agree on a policy of equal participation in meetings, rotate who starts, keep contributions short and sweet, and resolve conflict quickly.
7. **Commonality:** Face one another, use commonality in demeanour, energy and tone of voice to set the agenda, acknowledging diversity as the norm.

Technology and people: the top 10 impacts in the sales world

I've often pondered the topic of technology and how it impacts good leadership, especially when it comes to understanding why some organisations and their sales teams perform better than others. So, how does technology help to drive sales teams, and what are the roles that different generations play?

To be an effective sales leader today, understanding how technology influences people and recognising generational differences within teams are crucial. Technology has significantly transformed the role of traditional salespeople in several ways and, with the impact and capacity of AI growing every day, will continue to do so. Leaders must adapt sales strategies and coaching methods for different generations to connect effectively with a diverse audience. Here are 10 points to consider:

1. **Access to information:** Salespeople now have a vast amount of information about prospects and customers. Tools like Customer Relationship Management (CRM) systems and social media platforms provide insights into behaviour, preferences and purchase history, allowing tailored pitches and re-marketing to existing customers.

2. **Automation and efficiency:** Automation tools streamline sales processes, freeing up time for relationship-building. Email marketing automation, chatbots, and AI-driven customer service enhance efficiency, and are all designed to save time.

3. **Enhanced communication:** Video conferencing, instant messaging and social media enable personal interactions regardless of location. Real-time demonstrations and support are possible in even the remotest of locations.

4. **Data-driven decision making:** Analysing sales data and customer feedback empowers informed decisions. This data-driven approach improves targeting and conversion rates.

5. **Social selling:** Platforms like LinkedIn, Twitter and Facebook help sales professionals engage with prospects, build their brand and establish trust before formal sales processes. After-sales

follow-up is also a crucial factor when using these platforms to gather endorsements and testimonials.

6. **Virtual and augmented reality:** These technologies, although still the development stage, allow immersive product experiences. They are particularly effective for real estate, automotive and retail industries, not to mention role-playing gaming, or gamification of selling.

7. **E-Learning and training:** Online courses and webinars provide continuous learning opportunities, keeping salespeople updated on techniques and trends.

8. **Enhanced customer experience:** Integrated platforms offer a unified view of the customer journey, enabling personalised interactions and recommendations.

9. **Remote selling:** Virtual selling, fuelled by digital tools, connects sales teams with global prospects as well as suppliers to use for demonstration purposes.

10. **Challenges and adaptations:** While technology brings advantages, salespeople must adapt to new tools and remain flexible.

Number 10 is the most telling when considering what is happening around us and our teams. Coaching different generations in sales teams today requires a nuanced approach. There is no cookie-cutter method. While technology is streaking ahead, *people* are still the most critical factor in sales, and understanding how to deal with them helps navigate these technology impacts in the marketplace.

If you are struggling, try some of these strategies with multi-generational teams you may lead:

1. **Understand generational differences:** Recognise that each generation – Baby Boomers, Gen X, Millennials, Gen Z – has unique communication styles, work preferences and motivations. This

means to be successful you need to tailor your coaching methods based on these differences.

2. **Flexible communication:** Adapt your coaching style to match the preferred communication channels of each generation. Some prefer face-to-face meetings (Boomers and Gen X), while others (Millennial) might respond better to virtual communication or instant messaging.

3. **Feedback preferences:** Understand how different generations prefer to receive feedback. For instance, Baby Boomers may appreciate direct, in-person feedback, while Millennials might be more receptive to regular check-ins via email or video call.

4. **Emphasise skill development:** Focus on skill-building rather than just performance metrics. Provide training opportunities, workshops and resources to enhance their abilities. Consider e-learning platforms for continuous development.

5. **Mentoring and reverse mentoring:** Encourage cross-generational mentoring by creating buddy systems in-house or in-store. Experienced salespeople can mentor younger team members, while younger employees can offer insights into technology and social media.

6. **Recognition and rewards:** Tailor recognition and rewards to resonate with each generation. Some may value public praise, while others prefer private acknowledgment or tangible incentives. Either way, this is a principal factor in driving the success and esteem of the team.

7. **Work-life balance:** COVID made us realise and recognise that work–life balance priorities vary across generations. Be flexible with schedules and consider remote work options where feasible.

8. **Stay current with technology:** Keep up to date with technology trends. Understand how different generations use tools like CRM systems, social media and virtual meeting platforms.

9. **Lead by example:** Demonstrate the desired behaviours and work ethic. Show that you value diversity and appreciate the strengths each generation brings to the team. Fostering this collaboration across different generations in the workplace is essential for a harmonious and productive environment, especially when challenged with technological advancements. Acknowledging that different generations have varying levels of comfort with technology is the first step, followed by providing training and support to ensure everyone can effectively use the digital tools they need.

Remember that a steely focus on shared goals and recognition of individual strengths help transcend generational differences. When everyone is working towards a shared purpose, collaboration becomes more natural. This also leads to professional development opportunities where workshops, seminars and mentorship programs can drive change and understanding. Fostering this style of collaboration involves understanding, respect and a willingness to learn from each other. So, if you find yourself in a room with different generations and where technology abounds, try these team exercises to get the ball rolling:

- Have each team member identify their top workplace values. Discuss commonalities and differences, emphasising mutual respect and understanding.
- Assign multi-generational members to work together on projects to draw out and expose different outlooks and communication styles for a deeper understanding of each other.
- Provide technology training sessions such as workshops or lunch-and-learn sessions to help the different generations understand each other's perspectives. Address digital literacy gaps and promote technology adoption through experimentation and first-hand practical engagement/use of the new tools.

- The most popular by far – and the most effective: Do don't make it look like work. Offer casual team-building events through organised activities that encourage communication and collaboration in a relaxed setting. These can include team lunches, outings or creative challenges.

Remember, technology is here to stay, so creating an inclusive environment with your best people, no matter what age they are, involves active effort to bridge the generational differences.

Changing methodologies and diversity

As technology evolves, so do salespeople and their methods. The constant factor in sales has always been people – both those being sold to and the salespeople themselves.

To be an effective sales leader today, it's crucial to understand how technology influences people and, more importantly, how generational differences within sales teams play out in a business context.

Recognising the diverse aspects of people and their sales techniques is essential. Leaders must adapt their sales strategies and coaching methods for different generations to help them connect more effectively with a diverse audience.

The best example of segmentation and generational focus in sales and customer strategy that I have encountered was during a visit to Best Buy in the US. I saw that the US was far ahead in designing store layouts tailored to specific customer types. They based these designs on shopping frequency, ethnicity, demographic spending and detailed analysis of major sales segments across various product categories. This data-driven approach led to stores being named according to their customer profiles.

For instance, Best Buy had what they called 'Jill' stores. 'Jill' was the primary decision maker in her family, with two children and a professional husband; she was often described as a 'soccer mom'. She was middle-income and task-oriented, had a participative learning style and valued professional advice despite conducting thorough research herself.

Salespeople had to be particularly knowledgeable and socially aware when serving her, as she was well-educated and well-informed. Once her children were older, she returned to work and excelled professionally.

Stores designed for her designation were easy to navigate, the displays were appealing, with softer colour palettes, and the products very easily demonstrated, with time-effective considerations taken into account regarding getting in and out of the store. While this description might seem outdated today, it reflects how Best Buy approached retail in the late 1990s. You get the general idea.

Today's CRM systems and AI-driven tools are revolutionising business growth by screening millions of customers online and data mining various types of information for remarketing purposes. As someone who values personal connections, I believe that people buy from people before they buy products.

While I won't delve into the Silent Generation, also known as the Builders (those born 1925–1945), I will focus on people born from 1946 onwards – Baby Boomers, and Generations X, Y and Z. Let's look at how to effectively manage and lead multi-generational teams in this technologically advanced era of rapid growth.

Incentive programs for multi-generational teams

Putting together what we know about these four generations – Boomers, Gen X, Millennial and Gen Z – designing an effective sales incentive program for a multi-generational sales team requires balancing the diverse motivations, preferences and values of each group. There are some key principles and specific strategies to create an inclusive and motivating program.

Here are the 5 key principles:

- **Flexibility:** Offer a variety of incentives to cater to different preferences.
- **Transparency:** Ensure the program is clear and fair to all participants.

- **Personalisation:** Allow for individualised goals and rewards.
- **Recognition:** Acknowledge achievements in ways that resonate with each generation.
- **Professional Development:** Include opportunities for growth and learning.

Now, let's look at the major defining strategies for each generation.

- **Boomers:** Monetary rewards – offer cash bonuses and financial incentives.
- **Gen X:** Career advancement – provide clear paths for promotion and professional development.
- **Millennial:** Experiential rewards – provide travel opportunities, experiences or unique events.
- **Gen Z:** Work flexibility – offer remote work options and flexible hours.

Putting it all together, a comprehensive sales incentive program for a multi-generational team looks like this:

Monetary and non-monetary rewards combinations

- Bonuses – Performance-based cash bonuses for achieving sales targets
- Gift cards and vouchers – For popular stores or restaurants
- Travel incentives – All-expenses-paid trips for top performers
- Extra vacation days – For meeting or exceeding sales goals

Professional development

- Training programs – Access to workshops, courses and certifications
- Mentorship opportunities – Pairing newer employees with experienced mentors
- Leadership programs – For those interested in management roles

Recognition programs

- Monthly awards – Such as 'Salesperson of the Month' with public recognition
- Annual ceremonies – To celebrate major milestones and achievements
- Peer recognition – Platforms where colleagues can acknowledge each other's accomplishments

Wellness and social responsibility

- Health and wellness programs – Gym member-ships, wellness retreats, or health incentives
- Volunteer days – Paid days off for volunteering with chosen charities

There is no perfect answer, but considering the unique motivations and preferences of each generation, you can design a sales incentive program that drives performance and keeps your entire sales team engaged and satisfied.

Coaching multi-generational personalities

Gen Z – Wendy

'Wendy' – typically born between 1997 and 2012 – requires understanding, as her distinct characteristics, values and work preferences are born from the digital womb she was developed from. Gen Z individuals are 'digital natives'. They value authenticity and seek meaningful work, so effectively coaching a Gen Z professional in a business setting revolves around being authentic and have some digital fingerprint to leverage from. Here are some tips:

1. Wendy is highly proficient with technology and social media. She seeks genuine and transparent interactions and is always looking for meaningful work that aligns with her values. Wendy has

an entrepreneurial mindset, values innovation and appreciates diversity and inclusivity in the workplace.

2. Provide opportunities for growth and learning through access to online courses, workshops and training programs where she can build her skills. Encourage the focus on both soft and hard skills relevant to her role and career goals, clearly outlining potential career paths and opportunities for advancement.
3. Leveraging her technological skills in projects that utilise her comfort with digital tools and platforms will stimulate and encourage Wendy to bring innovative ideas and solutions to the table.
4. Align her work with purpose and values, making sure you include her in mission-driven projects where she can connect her tasks to the organisation's mission and values.

Here are some practical steps to help her at work:

1. Develop a customised Wendy-coaching plan, making sure there are clear, achievable goals and milestones, including opportunities for skill development and career growth.
2. Regular check-ins, such as for other team members, are critical but in Wendy's schedule, bi-weekly or monthly meetings to review progress work better. Be constructive with feedback and celebrate small wins to keep her motivated, adjusting plans based on her progress and any changes in her career goals or job responsibilities.
3. Providing resources and sharing relevant articles, books or podcasts that align with her professional interests will help build your credibility with her, while offering access to industry conferences, webinars or networking events as your company's representative is a show of trust in her capability.

4. Lastly, provide opportunities for cross-functional projects to broaden her experience.

Effectively coaching Gen Z professionals like Wendy will help them achieve their career goals and encourage them to contribute positively to the organisation.

Millennial – Oliver

Coaching a Millennial, like Oliver, involves understanding their unique characteristics, values, and work preferences. Millennials, typically born between 1981 and 1996, are known for their tech-savviness, desire for meaningful work and preference for collaboration. Oliver loves his Apple devices and finally sold his BMX bike to his younger cousin. He believes that his friendship group is his best source of advice and information. Here are some strategies to effectively coach a Millennial like Oliver in business:

1. Recognise his proficiency with technology and social media. Appreciate his innovative ideas and fresh perspectives.
2. The best communication style toward Oliver is all about regular updates and maintaining open communication channels. He prefers constructive feedback rather than annual reviews.
3. Career development and growth is all about Oliver understanding potential career trajectories within the organisation for himself – and quickly!
4. Leveraging Oliver's technological savvy and encouraging him to use digital tools and platforms to enhance productivity is a must. Involve him in projects that utilise his technological skills and creativity and reap the rewards.
5. Provide timely recognition for his contributions and achievements using public forums or team meetings to celebrate his successes.

6. Align Oliver's tasks with the organisation's mission and values. He enjoys corporate social responsibility, so CSR initiatives and projects with a social impact are his bag.

7. Oliver loves cross-functional projects because it provides him with opportunities to work on cross-functional teams to broaden his skills and meet new people.

Here are some practical ways to coach Oliver:

1. A customised coaching plan with specific objectives and timelines using technology as a basis of recording meetings like one-on-ones.

2. Regular check-ins are important, so schedule regular follow-up sessions with Oliver to track progress and adjust the plan as needed. He likes the attention from senior leaders.

3. Encouraging and fostering an environment that promotes the sharing of ideas and collaborative problem-solving with him taking the lead will reap massive benefits.

Oliver wants to fly out of the nest straight away like a baby eagle. That's great, but he does need care and mentoring first.

Gen X – Renee

Coaching a Gen X professional like Renee involves understanding their unique characteristics, work preferences and career aspirations. Gen X, typically born between 1965 and 1980, are known for their independence, resilience and adaptability. If you want to effectively coach a Gen X individual like Renee, try these steps:

1. Recognise the experience and skills she has developed over the years. Encourage her to contribute to strategic decisions, making her feel valued and respected.

2. Your communication style should be clear and straightforward, with regular updates and feedback to keep her informed and engaged.
3. Provide opportunities for Renee to work independently and make decisions, empowering her to take ownership of projects and tasks.
4. Leverage her technological savvy. She will be a quick adopter of the latest tools and platforms to keep her ahead in their field.
5. It's critical to encourage her participation in professional development programs, workshops and courses to help her outline clear career progression paths and growth opportunities within the organisation.
6. Work–life balance is critical, so be understanding of her family commitments and provide support where needed.
7. Provide opportunities for leadership roles and responsibilities and encourage Renee to mentor younger employees, sharing her knowledge and experience.
8. Involve Renee in corporate social responsibility initiatives, as many Gen Xers value social impact.

Making sure it all works:

1. Understand her current skills, goals and challenges through an initial meeting.
2. Develop a personalised coaching plan with specific objectives and timelines.
3. Scheduled regular follow-up sessions to track progress and adjust the plan as needed.
4. Provide access to resources such as workshops, reading materials and training sessions tailored to her needs.

With Renee, it's all about fostering an inclusive environment to get the best out of her. This approach will help her to achieve her career goals and contribute meaningfully to the organisation.

The Baby Boomer – Gary

Coaching someone like Gary involves understanding his unique characteristics, experiences and expectations. Baby Boomers, typically born between 1946 and 1964, have distinct professional and personal values shaped by historical events and societal changes. They have a directive style of leadership, with a structured learning style and tend to be thinkers.

Here are some strategies to effectively coach a baby boomer like Gary:

1. Respect his experience and knowledge; make Gary feel included and valued by consulting him on important decisions.
2. Gary appreciates straightforward and clear communication and values in-person meetings or phone calls over digital communication.
3. Address technological gaps. Offer training sessions to help Gary become comfortable with modern technologies, being patient and understanding about his learning curve with digital tools.
4. Leverage Gary's strengths. Encourage him to mentor younger employees, leveraging his wealth of experience.
5. Align with his values; Gary values hard work, dedication, loyalty and how they fit into the long-term goals of the company.
6. Offer flexible working hours or part-time options if he is transitioning to retirement.
7. Offer recognition and constructive feedback on a regular basis, acknowledging Gary's achievements and contributions to the team.

Practical steps you can use to help get the most from Boomers include:

1. Understanding their current skills, goals and challenges through an initial meeting.
2. Developing a personalised coaching plan that includes specific objectives and timelines.
3. Scheduling regular follow-up sessions to track progress and adjust their plan as needed.
4. Providing resources such as workshops, reading materials and training sessions.
5. Encouraging them to share their knowledge and experience with the team, fostering a collaborative environment.

The key is respecting Gary's experience and helping him to continue contributing meaningfully to the organisation. Do not discriminate based on age!

Gary, Renee, Oliver and Wendy will all live and work in harmony if, as a leader, you curate meetings carefully and understand what each person wants to achieve.

The psychology of winning

Winning in sales management requires a blend of empathy, strategy and resilience. It encompasses several critical aspects that contribute to successful sales. I call it the 'GO SCHEDULE'. Let's break it down.

G. Goal and Motivation Alignment

Sales teams thrive when their goals align with their organisational objectives. Managers should inspire and motivate their teams by emphasising the impact of their work.

Intrinsic motivation (personal fulfillment) and extrinsic motivation (rewards and recognition) both play a role.

O. Obligation to building rapport and trust

Salespeople must establish rapport with prospects by actively listening, empathising and demonstrating genuine interest. Trust-building techniques include active communication, transparency and consistency.

S. Self-confidence and a positive mindset

Sales professionals need a strong self-concept and unwavering confidence. Believing in their abilities and maintaining a positive mindset helps them overcome rejection and persist in their efforts. Self-affirmations, visualisation and goal setting contribute to a winning mentality.

C. Continuous learning and skill development

Top sales professionals never stop learning. They stay updated on industry trends, refine their techniques and seek feedback. Training programs, workshops and mentorship contribute to ongoing growth.

H. Handling objections and rejections

Rejections are inevitable in sales. Successful salespeople view objections as opportunities to address concerns and build stronger connections

E. Embracing resilience and adaptability

Sales environments change rapidly. Resilient salespeople bounce back from setbacks, learn from failures, and adapt their strategies. Flexibility and agility are essential traits for winning in sales.

D. Data-driven decision making

Sales managers analyse data to identify patterns, optimise processes and make informed decisions. Metrics like conversion rates, lead quality and pipeline velocity guide choices.

U. Understanding customer behaviour

Effective sales managers recognise that customers are not just rational decision makers. Emotions, biases and social influences play a significant role in their purchasing decisions. By understanding buyer psychology, sales teams can tailor their approaches to resonate with customer needs, desires and pain points.

L. Leveraging social proof and scarcity

Social proof (e.g., testimonials) influences prospects. Highlighting successful outcomes builds credibility. Scarcity (limited offers, exclusive deals) creates urgency and encourages action.

E. Effective communication skills

Sales managers emphasise the importance of clear communication, active listening, asking open-ended questions and adapting communication styles. Non-verbal cues such as body language also impact communication effectiveness.

By mastering these skills, you will thrive in sales capability!

The '3 Cs' of talent management and the '7 Cs' of communication

The '3 Cs' of talent management and the '7 Cs' of communication in business are the forces behind success. Commitment, Capability and Concentration make up the sweet spot of performance management, ensuring leaders get the most traction with their teams.

Commitment is your approach to work, where you demonstrate ownership, exhibit attitude and demonstrate emotional management and sustained willpower to see through the tasks and activities of your role with excellence.

Capability is how you demonstrate what you can do, showing through your current performance how you apply knowledge and relevant experience to the success of the team and business.

Concentration is all about having articulated goals, directional determination and clarity on the 'Ws' – Who, What, Why, When and Where.

On the other hand, Clarity, Correctness, Consideration, Courtesy, Completeness, Conciseness and Concreteness are the seven Cs of communication that will ensure your message reaches the audience clearly, accurately and with courtesy. Having a grip on these ten Cs is a surefire road to success in what you do and how you communicate it.

Change x 3

Investing in your employees' talent is crucial to the success of any business. It doesn't matter if you're online, in a shop or providing a service, having a team that can make quality decisions on your behalf is essential.

To ensure your team is equipped to handle any challenge, it's important to assess their impact, effectiveness and efficiency. The goal is to identify where improvements in your talent pool would make the biggest difference in becoming a world-class market leader.

Do you have a 'talentship' – a people philosophy that establishes the key components of the team you have in your organisation? It's a question worth asking.

Change in your business can come from many different sources, but who drives those changes?

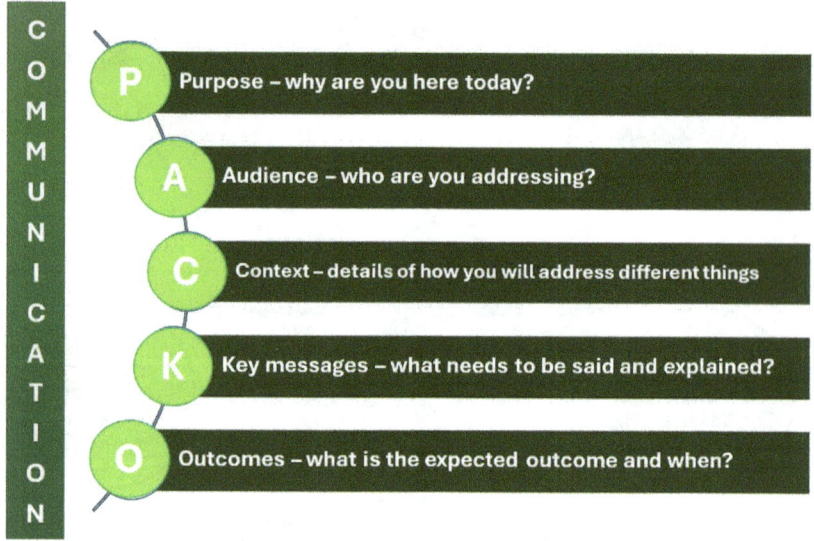

Effective communication and presentation skills

Effective communication skills are vital for success in any leadership role, and this includes giving a presentation. At some point in your career, you will be called upon to deliver a formal presentation, whether it's to executives, clients or your team. Whether you're presenting to a large audience or one-on-one, in-person or virtually, solid presentation skills matter. Even the most experienced presenters may need to fine-tune their skills to keep up with changing expectations.

This is why I recommend the PACKO acronym for preparing any presentation. It covers the 'Who, What, Where, When and Why' of the presentation skills space, ensuring you deliver well-crafted and on-point information every time. I picked up this technique through a course I completed, and it has been a game-changer for me. It's a simple approach but worth its weight in gold.

Remember, mastering presentation skills is key to succeeding in today's fast-paced business world.

Smart and fast goal setting

I was discussing goal setting recently with a regular at a coffee shop where I sometimes get my morning coffee. It's a small café across from the train line where I get on and off to get to the city. I'm a hit-and-miss sort of person, but this individual is always there, and we always exchange pleasantries.

This particular morning, our casual discussion turned into an in-depth conversation. We were sitting outside drinking our coffee when he began to quiz me about my current employment situation. We started talking about what goals we had for the future. I was guessing he had none, as he seemed quite positive about 'doing nuttin'' as he explained to me several times while laughing to himself. Then he totally surprised me.

"You've got SMART goals," he said. "You know what that means? *Specific* – being targeted in your approach. *Measurable* – you can get an indication of progress. *Achievable* – one must be aware of what they want to achieve. *Relevant* – have all the resources you need to complete the tasks. *Timely/timebound* – what is the deadline?"

Then he suggested the following:

- Frequently discuss your goals with someone close to you so they can hold you accountable to yourself.
- Be ambitious and tackle major targets you thought you might never get the opportunity to tackle. This is critical to your personal development.

- Be simplistic in your approach with an eye on the detail, so things are easy to explain.
- Be transparent enough so if you had the chance to tell someone what you were trying to achieve, they could understand it quickly.

He then went on to give me the following advice: you need to have a rhetoric with your soul when it comes to developing yourself, so make sure your artistic and creative juices are inspired and activated when setting your future plans. Nurture the steps to make sure the change is memorable, make it stick for good and then devote every minute of the day to achieving it.

Make sure there is a collaborative element to your plans so you can ensure that you connect with others as you progress. Limit how much you take on, because you can only serve one or two masters –you and your goals – when making change.

Lastly, ensure that your emotional state allows you to feel and be encouraged by the small changes you notice as you begin to commit to bettering yourself, so that when you complete your first set of goals in your rebirth, you truly appreciate the distance you've come.

Just one disclaimer though, he reminded me. "As the master of your destiny, you can refine and make changes on the speed or success of your progress. It's all about being smart, fast and clear!"

I paid for his coffee and thanked him. For me, his advice served as a great refresher.

The power of great storytelling

Once, in a meeting, I witnessed the power of storytelling in driving change. Two consultants were tasked with centralising a national pricing policy, a hot topic, with constituents from all states present. One consultant took the 'rip the Band-Aid off' approach, while the other told a story about a small village facing a similar challenge.

He likened his proposed solution to the proverb 'Give a man a fish and you feed him for a day. Teach a man to fish, and you feed him for a lifetime'. In other words, he stressed the importance of providing the people who worked for the company sustainable skills and knowledge rather than simply issuing 'quick-fix' directives with little thought for the long term.

The second consultant's storytelling technique, with its rhythmical musical cadence and memorable characters, effectively conveyed the case for change, while his methodology, which included investing in a comprehensive staff training program and bringing in experts to teach the team more effective skills and techniques, resulted in a successful long-term solution and sustainable growth for the company.

In the end, most of the room was willing to try the second approach. The moral of the story? Conveying change is all about the story and context, not just brute force. Reading the people in the room and having a genuine belief in what you are doing are also critical.

The 9-box Leadership and Matrix

Are you struggling with talent and leadership assessment in your organisation? Succession planning is hard enough without any means of tracking team members and teams. Luckily, there is a universal tool available to help.

The 9-box matrix is designed to give you a solid guide to managing expectations of team members. By closely aligning talent management and leadership initiatives to where they add the most value, you can make informed decisions about your team members' potential for growth and promotion.

Job description on a page

As a proponent of simplifying things in business, I believe in the power of distilling job descriptions down to a single page for reference. Just like having a strategy on a page for the team to refer to, a job description on a page serves the greater good of focusing a team member so they can grow in their role and deliver value.

When engaging in one-on-one conversations with team members, having their job description on hand can be a game changer. This allows

9 - BOX ASSESSMENT

GROWING TALENT
Development & Promotability
(Consider the following questions for everyone)
- If they are not currently meeting expectations (Capability), where are they in the other areas (Commitment & Concentration)?
- If they are currently meeting expectations, what development actions (anchored to Commitment and Concentration) could be leveraged to enhance and grow the employee?
- Is a 360 relevant?
- What other roles (lateral and promotion) might be an option for this employee? Today? Soon? Long term?
- What does the employee want?
- What dominant skills are highly valued by the organisation?
- Is there a back-fill in place for this person?

ASSESSING TALENT
Development & Possibilities
(Consider your approach to everyone)
- Share the individual's 9-box score.
- Everyone should have a feedback session that includes a formalised STOP/START/CONTINUE.
- Develop action list to follow up on (for leader and the direct report).
- Utilise the "C" frame to help the individual understand how talent is being viewed holistically, beyond the 9-box.
- If the individual is meeting expectations, schedule a time to sit down and complete an independent review of their performance. If the employee is not meeting expectations, begin the gap management/under performance process.

PERFORMANCE

	BELOW	MEETS	EXCEEDS
EXCEEDS (A)	**A3 AT RISK** — Leadership behaviour improvement required by individual	**A2** — Team member recognition by management	**A1** — Individual bonus or reward. Best in class team member highly promotable
MEETS (B)	**B3 AT RISK** — Leadership behaviour improvement required by individual	**B2** — Team member recognition by management	**B1** — Team member recognition by management
BELOW (C)	**C3 AT RISK** — On the way out if no improvement is made in 30 days	**C2 AT RISK** — Performance Improvement required by individual	**C1 RE INTERVIEW CANDIDATE** — Performance Improvement required by individual

LEADERSHIP

Ask what the team member should stop, start and continue doing for improvement in their role

- 🟠 What are the things you should stop doing to improve performance?
- 🟡 What are the things you should start doing to continue to improve performance?
- 🟢 What should you keep doing to improve performance?

Harnessing Leadership, Ideas, People and Strategy

you to reflect on their performance, understand their current routine and ensure that they are aligned with the company's overall vision. It can also be a helpful educational tool for staff development, providing a concise and clear communication when reviewing performance in appraisals.

In my experience, having a job description on one page has been crucial in giving a balanced one-on-one and understanding everyone's role in the organisation. It can be used in three different ways: as a resource tool for up-and-comers and new team members; in conjunction with one-on-one weekly interviews; and as a potential tool for concise and clear communication when reviewing performance in appraisals.

Acronyms to remember

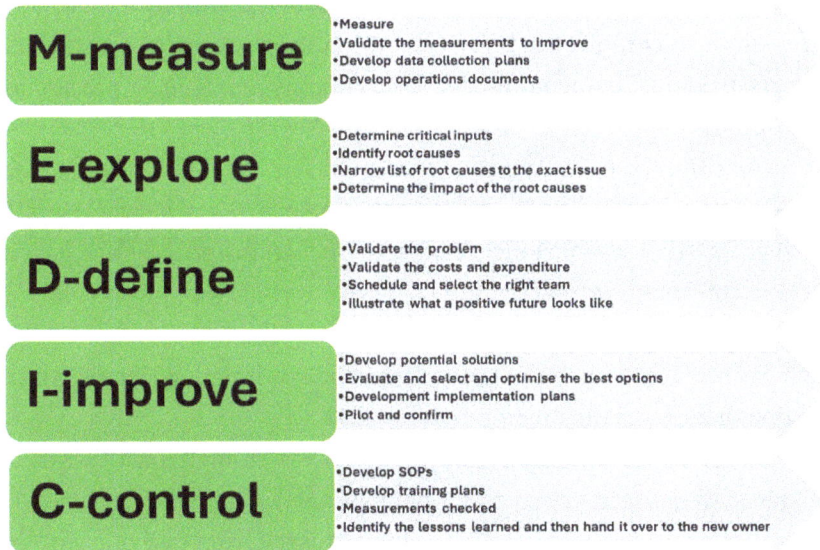

Kaizen is a Japanese business philosophy that emphasises continuous improvement and involves all employees. At its core, Kaizen empowers individuals to effect change and improve productivity through teamwork and regular meetings.

The five principles of Kaizen are:

1. know your customer;
2. let it flow;
3. go to see the people;
4. empower people; and
5. be transparent.

To simplify the concept of remembering the process elements behind Kaizen, I often create acronyms to help me recall the information more easily. For example, MEDIC stands for Measure, Explore, Define, Improve and Control – the basics of Kaizen thinking. It works for me as it paints the picture of a doctor working through a prognosis of a patient's aliments, and then issuing a set of steps to remedy the problem. This simple technique can be a valuable addition to your business thinking arsenal when being inundated with copious amounts of information in your role.

Transitioning from People to Strategy in our LIPS framework bridges the importance of nurturing talent with the necessity of a clear roadmap to success. After establishing strong, engaged teams, and fostering a culture of continuous growth, the focus shifts to channelling this collective energy and talent into actionable strategies. This pivot acknowledges that a motivated team is the foundation, but a well-defined strategy is the engine that moves the organisation forward.

The transition emphasises aligning people's strengths with organisational goals, ensuring every team member not only understands but also feels part of the larger mission. It's about moving from individual potential to collective purpose, crafting strategies that capitalise on your team's unique capabilities, insights, and innovative potential. This alignment between people and strategy is critical to build resilience, adapt to market shifts, and drive sustainable growth. Let's have a good look at the 'S' in the LIPS framework: Strategy.

5. STRATEGY

Strategy is the most common word we hear in business every day. This is no wonder, when the concept of strategy has been pivotal in human history, guiding decisions in warfare, politics and business. Originating from a military context, the evolution of strategy has profoundly influenced contemporary business practices, shaping how organisations navigate competitive landscapes and achieve their goals.

The term 'strategy' derives from the Greek word *strategos* meaning 'generalship'. In ancient times, strategy was primarily associated with military leadership and the art of warfare. Sun Tzu's *The Art of War*, written around the 5th century BC, is one of the earliest texts on strategic thinking, emphasising the importance of planning, flexibility and understanding one's adversaries.

As societies evolved, the application of strategy extended beyond the battlefield. During the Renaissance, figures such as Niccolò Machiavelli contributed to strategic thought in politics with works such as *The Prince*, advocating for cunning and pragmatism in statecraft. The Industrial Revolution further transformed strategic thinking as businesses grew in complexity. Pioneers like Frederick Winslow Taylor introduced scientific management principles, emphasising efficiency and productivity.

His ideas, developed in the late 19th and early 20th centuries, were groundbreaking at the time and laid the foundation for modern management practices. Taylor's principles of scientific management include the following concepts that are still in play today.

1. **Scientific job analysis:** Taylor proposed that work should be studied scientifically to identify the most efficient way to perform tasks. This involved breaking down tasks into smaller components, timing each element and determining the best methods and tools for each job. This analysis aimed to eliminate unnecessary motions and optimise productivity.

2. **Standardisation of work:** Once the best methods for performing tasks were identified, Taylor proposed that these methods should be standardised and implemented across the organisation. Standardisation ensured consistency, quality and efficiency in the execution of tasks.

3. **Selection and training of workers:** Taylor emphasised the importance of selecting the right workers for the right jobs based on their skills and capabilities. He also advocated for providing workers with the proper training to perform their tasks efficiently according to scientifically determined methods.

4. **Cooperation between management and workers:** Taylor believed that cooperation between management and workers was essential for achieving efficiency. He proposed a system where managers would plan and supervise work, while workers would execute the tasks. This division of labour aimed to maximise productivity by leveraging the strengths of both management and workers.

5. **Division of work:** Taylor introduced the concept of dividing work between managers and workers. Managers were responsible for planning, organising and overseeing the work, while workers were responsible for executing the tasks. This division allowed managers to focus on improving work methods and processes, while workers concentrated on their specific tasks.

6. **Incentive wage system:** Taylor advocated for a differential piece-rate system, where workers were paid based on their productivity.

This system provided financial incentives for workers to meet and exceed performance standards, motivating them to work more efficiently.

7. **Task allocation:** Taylor's system involved assigning specific tasks to workers based on their abilities and expertise. This specialisation ensured that each worker performed tasks for which they were best suited, further enhancing efficiency and productivity.

Taylor's scientific management principles aimed to transform the workplace by applying scientific methods to management practices. Although some aspects of his approach have been criticised for treating workers as mere components of a machine, his ideas significantly influenced the development of modern management theories and practices, emphasising efficiency, productivity and the systematic study of work processes.

The mid-20th century marked a significant shift as strategic thinking became formalised within the business domain. Scholars such as Alfred D. Chandler Jr. highlighted the importance of organisational structure and strategic planning in his seminal work, *Strategy and Structure* (1962). Chandler argued that a company's strategy should dictate its organisational structure, a concept that re-shaped corporate management.

The rise of strategic management as a discipline brought forward various models and frameworks, such as Michael Porter's Five Forces analysis, which helps businesses understand the competitive forces that shape their industry. The Boston Consulting Group's growth-share matrix provided a tool for portfolio management, guiding investment decisions based on market growth and relative market share.

In today's globalised and rapidly changing business environment, strategy is more critical than ever. Here are some ways in which strategy has become indispensable in business and why it plays such an important role in the development of leadership and people and helps in creating an innovative environment in business.

- **Navigating complexity**

  Businesses operate in increasingly complex environments with technological advancements, regulatory changes and shifting consumer preferences. A well-crafted strategy helps organisations navigate these complexities, identify opportunities and mitigate risks.

- **Competitive advantage**

  Strategy enables businesses to differentiate themselves from competitors. By leveraging unique resources and capabilities, companies can create sustainable competitive advantages, ensuring long-term success.

- **Resource allocation**

  Effective strategy guides the allocation of resources, ensuring that investments are made in areas with the highest potential for return. This prioritisation is crucial for maximising profitability and growth.

- **Alignment and direction**

  A clear strategy aligns the efforts of employees and stakeholders, providing a shared vision and direction. This cohesion is vital for driving collective action towards common goals.

- **Adaptability and resilience**

  Strategic thinking fosters adaptability, allowing businesses to respond proactively to changes in the external environment. This resilience is essential for maintaining stability and continuity in the face of disruptions.

The history of strategy reflects its transformation from ancient military practices to a cornerstone of modern business management. As organisations face unprecedented challenges and opportunities, the importance of strategic thinking cannot be overstated. By understanding and applying strategic principles, businesses can achieve sustained success and remain competitive in a dynamic world. So, let's quickly look at the various components of successful strategic planning.

Understanding the components of strategic planning

Strategic planning is the process by which an organisation defines its direction and makes decisions on allocating its resources to pursue this direction. It involves setting long-term goals, identifying the necessary actions to achieve those goals and mobilising resources to execute the actions. The more you break down the details of what must be done to deliver transformational change and results, the better the strategic document is for your organisation and senior leadership to absorb.

- A. **The role of vision and mission statements:** These statements define the organisation's purpose and primary objectives. The vision statement describes what the organisation aspires to become in the future, while the mission statement outlines the organisation's fundamental purpose and activities. I always like to keep this process very simple, so it's easy to explain to people and easy for them to understand.

    Based on the vision and mission statements, **S**pecific, **M**easurable, **A**chievable, **R**elevant and **T**ime-bound (SMART) objectives can then be established to guide the organisation's efforts. This involves understanding, discussing and analysing internal and external environments to identify **S**trengths, **W**eaknesses, **O**pportunities and **T**hreats (SWOT analysis). This step is crucial for understanding the context in which the organisation operates.

- B. **Strategy formulation:** This involves developing a plan to achieve the set objectives. It includes deciding on the best courses of action, resource allocation and defining KPIs to measure progress.

C. **Implementation:** The formulated strategy is put into action. This requires effective communication, coordination and management of resources to ensure that all parts of the organisation are working towards the common goals.

D. **Evaluation and control:** Continuous monitoring and assessment of the strategy's effectiveness are essential. This involves tracking progress, measuring outcomes against KPIs and adjusting as needed to stay on course.

Leadership steps in strategy alignment

Consistent Review and Adjustment
Regularly reviewing and adjusting the strategy ensures that it remains relevant and aligned with the vision. This requires flexibility and adaptability in response to changing circumstances.

Leadership Involvement
Leaders at all levels should be involved in the strategic planning process to ensure that their insights and perspectives are considered. This fosters a sense of ownership and commitment to the strategy.

Clear Communication
The vision and mission must be clearly communicated to all members of the organisation. Everyone should understand the long-term goals and how their individual roles contribute to these goals.

Integrated Planning
Strategic planning should be integrated across all levels of the organisation. Departmental plans should align with the overall strategy, ensuring coherence and unity in efforts.

A successful strategy is one that aligns closely with the organisation's vision and mission. This alignment ensures that all strategic initiatives are directed towards achieving the overarching goals of the organisation. The easiest way to demonstrate this is through a series of steps leaders should take to achieve organisational alignment.

Adaptive strategies in business

In a rapidly changing business environment, the ability to adapt is critical. Adaptive strategy involves continuously monitoring the external environment and being prepared to make changes to the strategic plan as needed. Porter's Five Forces model, along with an extension of the SWOT planning exercise – the PESTLED model – can help leaders adjust and correct plans where necessary. Other ways leaders can do this is by regularly monitoring external factors such as market trends, technological advancements and regulatory changes to identify opportunities and threats.

Developing flexible strategies that can be adjusted quickly in response to new information or changing circumstances is the name of the game for agile and nimble organisations. In many instances, this may involve having contingency plans and being open to pivoting when necessary. This is done through careful scenario planning and various 'what if' exercises.

If you haven't heard of scenario planning, this is a strategic planning method used by organisations to anticipate and prepare for potential future events and conditions. It involves creating detailed and plausible scenarios based on a range of uncertainties, such as economic shifts, technological advancements, regulatory changes and social trends. These scenarios are not predictions; rather, they are explorations of different possible futures. By considering numerous scenarios, organisations can identify potential risks and opportunities, allowing them to develop flexible strategies that can be adapted as circumstances change.

This approach helps organisations build resilience and agility, as it encourages long-term thinking and proactive planning. Through scenario planning, decision makers can better understand the potential impacts of different developments and make informed choices that enhance their ability to respond to unexpected changes. Ultimately, scenario planning enables organisations to navigate uncertainty more effectively, ensuring they are better prepared for whatever the future may hold.

Agility is critical in ensuring that the organisation has processes and structures in place that allow for rapid decision making and implementation. This often involves decentralised decision making and empowering employees at all levels. By having a continuous learning environment and fostering a culture of continuous learning and improvement, where feedback is actively sought and used to refine strategies and processes, businesses can quickly navigate and avert possible disasters.

Leadership and strategic execution

Effective leadership is the driving force behind successful strategic execution. Leaders set the vision and direction of an organisation, ensuring that everyone understands the strategic goals and their role in achieving them. They inspire and motivate employees, fostering a sense of purpose and commitment. A leader's ability to communicate the strategy clearly and convincingly is crucial, as it aligns the organisation's efforts and resources towards common objectives, creating a cohesive and focused workforce.

Strategic execution involves translating strategic plans into actionable steps and ensuring these steps are implemented efficiently. Leaders play a pivotal role in this process by establishing clear priorities, allocating resources wisely, and setting measurable targets. They must also create a culture of accountability, where progress is regularly monitored and deviations are addressed promptly. Effective leaders are adept at identifying potential obstacles and devising solutions, ensuring that the strategy is executed smoothly and objectives are met.

Leaders must also be adaptable and resilient, capable of adjusting strategies in response to changing circumstances. This requires a continuous feedback loop where they gather insights from the implementation process and make the necessary adjustments. By fostering an environment of continuous improvement and encouraging innovation, leaders can ensure that strategic execution remains dynamic and responsive to both internal and external changes. Ultimately, strong leadership in strategic execution leads to sustained organisational success and a competitive edge in the marketplace.

Executing a strategy effectively requires meticulous planning, coordination and management. It involves translating strategic plans into actionable tasks and ensuring that all parts of the organisation are working towards the common goals. One of the best ways to do this is through a 'cascading strategy'. A cascading strategy is beneficial in aligning organisational objectives at all levels, ensuring that every department and team is working towards the same overarching goals.

This approach begins with the top-level strategic vision and progressively breaks it down into specific, actionable plans for each layer of the organisation. By doing so, it creates a clear line of sight from the executive leadership to individual employees, enhancing coherence and focus across the entire company. This alignment is vital for maintaining consistency in decision making and prioritising efforts that drive the organisation towards its strategic objectives.

Implementing a cascading strategy also fosters a sense of ownership and accountability among employees. When team members understand how their roles contribute to the broader goals of the organisation, they are more likely to be engaged and motivated. This connection between individual tasks and the company's mission encourages employees to take the initiative and perform their duties with greater commitment and enthusiasm. It also enables managers to track progress more effectively, as they can measure individual and team performance against specific targets that are directly linked to the company's strategic aims.

A cascading strategy enhances communication and collaboration within the organisation. By clearly defining and disseminating strategic priorities at every level, it reduces ambiguity and ensures that everyone is on the same page. This clarity facilitates better cross-functional collaboration, as teams can see how their efforts interrelate and support each other. It also allows for more effective feedback loops, where insights and challenges from different levels of the organisation can be communicated upward and incorporated into strategic adjustments. Ultimately, this dynamic and integrated approach to strategy execution drives organisational agility and long-term success.

Now that we understand that strategy and leadership are in constant motion, let's look at some of the key aspects of strategic execution to round out how important this aspect is in business.

Key aspects of strategic execution

One of the key aspects of strategic execution is clear and effective communication. Leaders must articulate the strategic vision and objectives in a way that is easily understood by all members of the organisation. This involves not just top-down communication but also creating channels for feedback and dialogue. Clear communication ensures that everyone understands their roles, responsibilities and how their individual contributions align with the broader organisational goals. Consistent messaging and transparency in sharing progress and challenges keep the team engaged and focused on executing the strategy effectively.

Another critical aspect is resource allocation. Successful strategic execution requires the appropriate allocation of financial, human and technological resources. Leaders must prioritise initiatives that align with the strategic goals and ensure that teams have the necessary tools and support to carry out their tasks. This involves careful planning and continuous monitoring to adjust resource distribution as needed. Efficient resource allocation helps to overcome obstacles, seize opportunities and maintain momentum towards achieving strategic objectives.

Lastly, performance management is essential for strategic execution. Establishing clear metrics and key performance indicators (KPIs) allows organisations to track progress and measure success against strategic goals. Regular reviews and assessments help to identify any deviations from the plan and enable timely corrective actions. Performance management also involves recognising and rewarding achievements, which motivates employees and reinforces their commitment to the strategic vision. By maintaining a focus on performance, organisations

Peter Sinodinos 133

Performance Management
Implementing a performance management system to track progress, measure outcomes, and provide feedback. This includes setting clear performance indicators and regularly reviewing them.

Risk Management
Identifying potential risks and developing strategies to mitigate them. This involves anticipating challenges and having contingency plans in place.

Communication
Maintaining open and effective communication channels to ensure that all stakeholders are informed about the progress and any changes to the strategy.

Resource Allocation
Ensuring that the necessary resources - financial, human, and technological - are allocated appropriately to support the execution of the strategy.

Operational Planning
Breaking down the strategic plan into detailed operational plans that outline specific actions, timelines, and responsibilities.

can ensure that their strategic initiatives stay on course and deliver the desired outcomes.

Continuous evaluation and control are also essential to ensure that the strategy remains effective and aligned with the organisation's goals. This involves regular monitoring of progress and making necessary adjustments. As mentioned, a Continuous Communication Loop assists in this area and you will see, from a series of posts I did on this topic on LinkedIn, how crucial it is. In the meantime, this simple explanation gives you a helicopter view of the important components of this part of the strategy curation.

Strategy and innovation

Within the LIPS framework, the relationship between strategy, innovation and ideas is foundational to the growth and competitiveness of an organisation. Strategy serves as the roadmap that guides an organisation towards its long-term goals, defining the direction and scope of its activities. Innovation, on the other hand, is the process of translating new ideas into products, services or processes that create value. Effective strategy must encompass innovation to remain relevant and adaptive in a rapidly changing market environment. Thus, the interplay between strategy and innovation ensures that an organisation not only sets a clear path but also continually evolves to meet emerging challenges and opportunities.

Ideas are the raw materials of innovation. They represent the creative sparks that can lead to groundbreaking products, services or improvements in processes. Without a steady flow of new ideas, innovation stagnates and organisations may struggle to keep up with their competitors. A well-formulated strategy should create an environment that encourages the generation and development of ideas. This involves fostering a culture of creativity, supporting research and development activities, and providing mechanisms for capturing and nurturing innovative concepts. By integrating idea generation into its strategic framework, an organisation ensures a constant influx of fresh perspectives and solutions.

Innovation acts as a bridge between ideas and strategic execution. Once promising ideas are identified, they need to be transformed into actionable initiatives that align with the organisation's strategic objectives. This transformation requires a structured approach to evaluating, refining and implementing ideas. Strategic innovation management involves assessing the potential impact of new ideas, aligning them with market needs and business goals, and allocating resources to bring them to fruition. By systematically integrating innovation into the strategic process, organisations can turn creative concepts into tangible outcomes that drive growth and competitive advantage.

The synergy between strategy, innovation and ideas ultimately leads to sustained success and differentiation in the marketplace. An organisation that strategically fosters innovation is better positioned to anticipate and respond to industry trends, customer demands and technological advancements. This proactive stance not only enhances the organisation's ability to innovate, but also ensures that its innovations are strategically aligned and impactful. In this dynamic interplay, strategy provides direction, ideas fuel creativity and innovation drives implementation, creating a virtual cycle that propels the organisation forward.

The following three strategic success models successfully demonstrate this approach.

1. **Amazon's** customer-centric strategy revolves around customer satisfaction. The company continuously innovates to enhance the customer experience, from its recommendation algorithms to its efficient logistics network. Amazon's strategic focus on customer-centricity has driven its success and made it a market leader.

2. **Tesla's** strategy is based on disruptive innovation in the automotive industry. By focusing on electric vehicles and renewable energy solutions, Tesla has positioned itself as a leader in sustainable technology. The company's strategic investments in R&D and its commitment to innovation have fuelled its rapid growth.

3. **Netflix's** ability to adapt its strategy in response to market changes has been key to its success. Initially a DVD rental service, Netflix then transitioned to a streaming model and invested heavily in original content. This adaptive strategy has enabled Netflix to stay ahead of its competitors and dominate the streaming industry.

Strategic planning and execution are fundamental to the success of any organisation. A well-defined strategy provides a roadmap for achieving long-term goals, while effective execution ensures that the strategy is translated into actionable tasks. Adaptive strategies, continuous evaluation and fostering innovation are crucial for staying competitive in a rapidly changing business environment.

By understanding and leveraging the inter-relationship between strategy, leadership, ideas and people, organisations can create a cohesive framework that drives sustained success. Leaders play a critical role in this process, providing vision, direction and support to ensure that all elements work together harmoniously. Investing in strategic planning and execution, fostering a culture of innovation, and focusing on continuous improvement and communication are key to building a resilient and successful organisation.

Following are some examples of recent blogs I shared covering the importance of strategy and a continuous communication loop to keep leaders and their teams on track.

The P.E.S.T.L.E.D. analysis method

Are you looking to take your business to the next level? A P.E.S.T.L.E.D. strategic analysis could be the answer. This framework examines external market factors such as Political, Economic, Social, Technological, Legal, Environmental, and Natural Disasters and Demographic. By understanding these influences, you can identify market trends that might impact your organisation's direction, performance and position in the marketplace. Used in tandem with a SWOT analysis, P.E.S.T.L.E.D. helps your organisation examine external factors that could influence opportunities and threats.

While it may seem like a lengthy process, taking the time to work through these frameworks is well worth it. By doing so, you can ensure that no stone is left unturned, and everything is exposed. Adding the ethical factor to the P.E.S.T.L.E.D. framework ensures that, from a governance point of view, your exposure to potential threats is minimised.

Don't let external factors impact your success. Take the time to conduct a detailed analysis and get to the bottom of everything that will impact you. With a solid understanding of your operating environment, industry and market, you'll be better equipped to overcome any challenges that come your way.

SWOT: Looking for the gaps

SWOT analysis is a great tool for identifying **S**trengths, **W**eaknesses, **O**pportunities and **T**hreats related to your business. It's a strategic planning technique that helps with decision-making processes and project planning. In other words, it's a type of situational analysis that deals with everything now and on a micro level.

If you're not familiar with SWOT analysis, it's designed for use in the initial stages of decision-making processes and can be used as a tool to assess the strategic position of your organisation. It's intended to identify internal and some external factors that are favourable and unfavourable for achieving the objectives of your organisation.

To get more clarity on the external factors, you can use a P.E.S.T.L.E.D. framework. Users of a SWOT analysis always ask and answer questions to derive information for each category to make the tool useful and identify their competitive advantage.

Keep in mind that SWOT has limitations, and some alternatives have been developed. However, when used in conjunction with other frameworks, it's a great way to get the ball rolling on strategy generation. Using SWOT analysis in the right way can help you identify gaps and opportunities in your analysis.

Volume mix and rate: The VMR index

During product and business reviews, variances against plan can cause intense discussions and passionate qualifications of a buyer's performance. Analysing product performance variances requires in-depth analysis, and finding the root cause is critical to the product lifecycle. But the window of time to unearth the cause of variances is short, and it usually occurs at the end of the month when things are most hectic.

Variance analysis often involves comparing existing metrics – but there's a better way to find the root cause of product performance. It's called a VMR index, and it centres around volume, mix and rate. 'Volume' refers to the amount of product sold or not sold, 'rate' refers to the price of the product, and 'mix' refers to the individual items' makeup.

I like to visualise VMR as a stereo deck with three dials, each with its specific purpose, and a read-out graph detailing the results. It's a useful mind tool to help me get to the crux of an issue when it comes to a product. VMR can be used in manufacturing, logistics and retail, and it's a great method for a mental check before diving deep into metrics. It's all about the impact on margin and gross profit, ideally impacting final EBIT results. Using this mental model when approaching product performance analysis sets you up for greater success down the track.

Business lifecycles

Understanding the business cycle is crucial for navigating the market's ups and downs, whether you're a small retail business or an entire country's economy. The cycle begins with growth, where positive factors such as sales, profits, wages and demand all rise. Then comes the peak, where businesses maximise growth, and ego can cloud strategic planning. The shrinking phase follows, where demand falls and prices start to decline. The business may hit rock bottom and need resuscitation. Finally, the revival stage begins, where strategic planning is crucial to pick up demand again.

Many factors can impact these lifecycles. Your strategic plans – and sticking to them and executing them well – are all critical for your success. Remember, tough times will come if you don't stay on top of your plans and customers, so keep your eye on the ball and stay ahead of the game.

The D.E.C.K.S. hypothesis

"It takes all the running you can do to keep in the same place." – The Red Queen said it best to Alice in *Through the Looking-Glass and what Alice Found There*.

This quote coined the business theory 'The Red Queen Hypothesis'. Essentially, if you don't keep running, you will fall behind. No matter what position you hold in your respective market, if you don't adapt, you'll die. Trying to stay ahead of the competition can be tiring, but you can flip it on its head by taking a calm and focused approach. Remember the Red Queen scenario with a simple acronym: D.E.C.K.S.

> **D.** Constantly look to **Differentiate** yourself from competitors by offering new products and high service standards from your team members.

- **E. Evolve** your thinking through research and foster an environment of innovation among the team, ensuring they are prepared to take calculated risks.
- **C.** Be **Competitive** and aware of the players and the trends in the market. Don't let them dictate your strategy. More importantly, adapt your strategy to overcome them.
- **K.** Be **Kinetic**. Keep moving, and don't sit still for long. Strike while the iron is hot when making changes to meet the market. Implement and refine.
- **S.** Have **Strategies**. While it may seem contradictory to what I have said previously, having an industry context where you assess every move will give you a better understanding of the next direction to take.

SPAMBOTS: My top eight strategies for success

I love strategy work. It challenges you to find solutions or explore new avenues you didn't know existed. As an old manager of mine used to say, overconfidence and arrogance can be the kiss of death. My epiphany came when trying to turn around organisations that had issues related to strategy and people. Let's face it, the two biggest things you can have in an organisation are a plan and people committed to it. Everything else tends to work itself out because of the planning and the collective strength of the bench that sits with you.

Here are some great statistics about strategy. Since 1958 right up until 2013, there have been approximately 81 different strategic frameworks developed in the world. From the Ansoff Matrix in 1958 to Transient Competitive Advantage 2013, these are digestible elements in strategy that I would encourage you to understand and to coach your teams in the thinking behind them. My top eight, and the ones you need to know to help you formulate good strategy in the future, are:

- SWOT;
- Porter's 5 Forces;

Peter Sinodinos 141

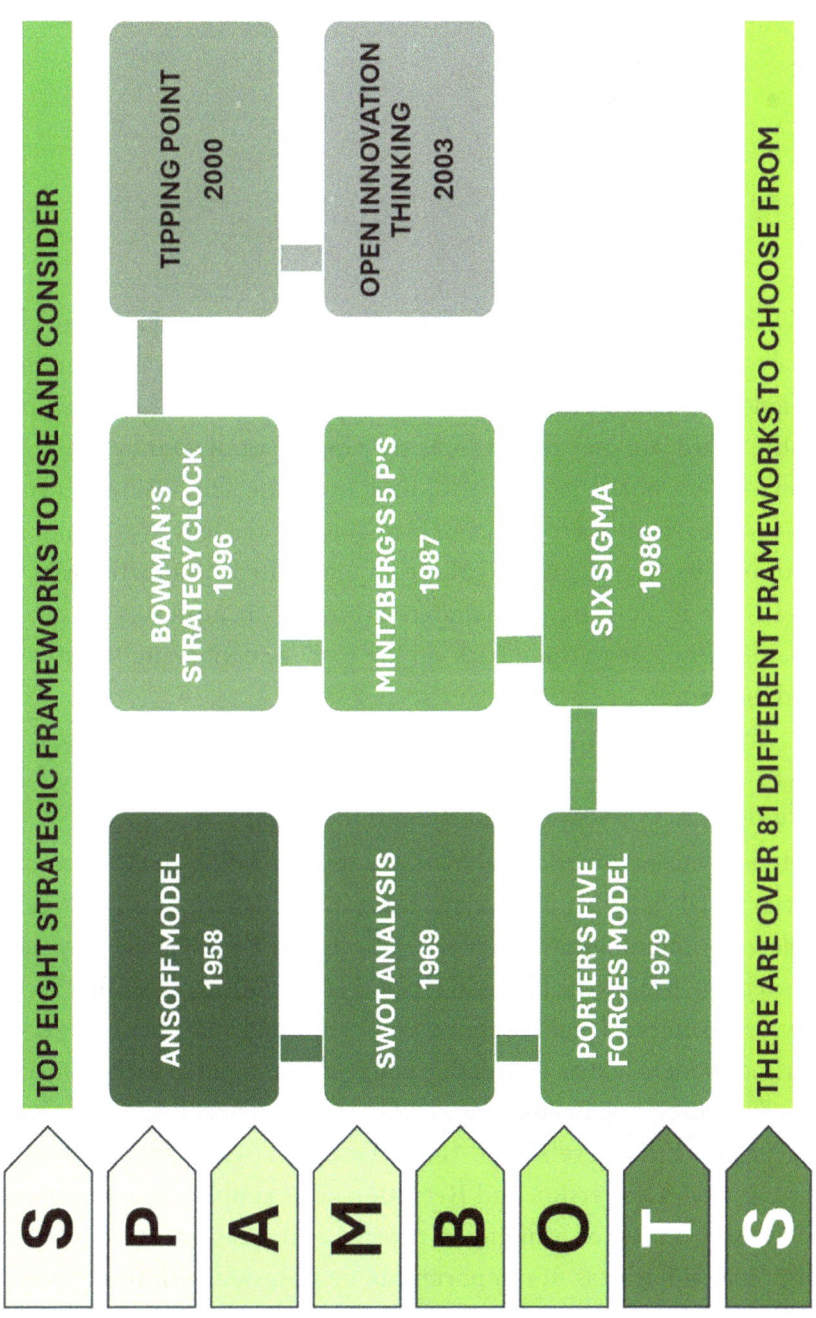

- Ansoff Model;
- Mintzberg's 5 Ps;
- Bowman's Strategy;
- Open Thinking;
- Tipping Point; and
- Six Sigma.

Remember, the selection of people and a systemised approach to a strategy is critical. One small mistake, such as overlooking something or ignoring signs of trouble, and, basically, you're toast. This also applies to the board you may report to, as they form part of your bench. If you don't have a board to report to, understanding the business owner's true wishes is critical for success. Good boards challenge your thinking, your proposed strategy and your team to excellence and will assist you to achieve it. Poor board members protect their positions within the board, putting everything back on the management team, the strategy and the people.

Investing in great people and paying strategy your dues is critical.

Acquisition, Conversion and Retention (ACR)

In today's business world, maintaining a strong relationship with customers is crucial. In my experience, the best way to do this is through personal follow-up communication. While AI-generated messaging may seem convenient, it lacks the personal touch that customers crave. That's why I always recommend making phone calls or meeting with clients in person. It's important to reassure them that you're still committed to their success.

Surprisingly, many businesses fail to follow up with clients or leads, leaving potential revenue on the table. That's why I focus on ACR: **A**cquisition, **C**onversion and **R**etention. This simple message reminds me to stay on top of bringing in revenue and creating future pipelines of potential business. It's important to be obsessed with this approach to business.

Peter Sinodinos 143

Prospect — Acquisition stage

- Create awareness, interest, decisions and action through above and under the line advertising, social – paid and organic, word of mouth, CRM software applications, customer feedback, mobile experience and advocate endorsements. Prospect starts to engage deeper with you. Capture details of prospect and any key intelligence to remember from the discussions with them.

Customer — Selling stage

- Product selection, ranging pricing, company values, brands available, company branding, trust in company, trust in salesperson, identifying the problem the customer has and solving it with your product, value equation, and the prospect prepared to pay for the product or service. Contact customer within 24 hours-36 hours of initial enquiry. Website used as a selling tool.

Client — Conversion stage

- Focus on customer lifetime value, validate and enhance the customer experience through hitting key dates and times promised, understand your customer and capture all their personal details, make them feel special, they pay for the product and or service. They buy from you again and are rewarded with better service. Satisfaction surveys and phone follow ups – 5 star google reviews requested.

Advocate — Retention stage

- Confidence in the service and company they deal with. Followed up through rewards programs and offers, as well as a physical call. If birthday information captured, then a personal call made. Social media remarketing and category extension offers sent to customer's email. Satisfaction surveys and phone 'follow ups'.

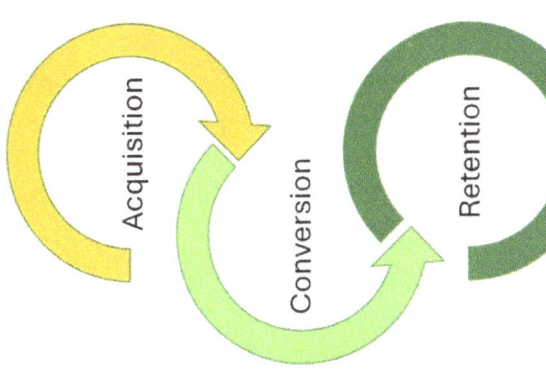

Ask yourself these questions to maintain good ACR in your business:

1. What process do I undertake to acquire customers outside of current streams?
2. How do I deliver a different point of view to retain customers' attention from the market?
3. What is the process to metamorphosise leads from a cold call to a warm lead?
4. What is the process for warm leads to decide to invest money in my services?

Remember, moving a prospect first to a customer, then a client and, finally, an advocate should always be the goal. No computer can do that for you – *you* are the key. People still need personal contact with someone, and it needs to be sincere, transparent and to the point.

Think ACR – it will take you far!

The 100-day plan

Are you starting a new role and want to make an impact in your first 100 days? Here are some tips to get you started and moving in the right direction.

Firstly, establish who's who in the zoo. Get to know everyone who will have a direct impact on you and your success starting out. Secondly, plan and take actions that create value and transformation – but not just for the sake of change. Thirdly, identify quick wins through your discovery process to give you the confidence they can be achieved. Lastly, communicate the change to the team, selecting your allies carefully.

Remember, it's all about the *team*. You need a coalition of willing advocates to campaign with you in the first 100 days. Taking this approach is sure to make your 100-day plan succeed.

Continuous problem solving

Are you tired of feeling stuck on the same 'solutions merry-go-round' when problems arise? Do you find that the more advice you get, the more confusing and overwhelming the situation becomes? If so, it's time to change your approach to problem-solving. By applying a continuous problem-solving process with clear steps, you can navigate next steps with less stress and more confidence. Here are eight steps to help you get started.

1. Identify the problem.
2. Gather information and data.
3. Analyse the data to find the root cause.
4. Generate potential solutions.
5. Select the best solution.
6. Plan implementation using a predict, prove, confirm process.
7. Test the solution and confirm the outcome.
8. Continuously evaluate and improve your problem-solving process.

Don't let problems overwhelm you. Take control with a clear problem-solving process.

Kaizen power

I mentioned the Kaizen philosophy in the previous chapter, but let's have a closer look at the concept. It's a Japanese term that means 'good change', and it emphasises continuous improvement through small, incremental changes every day. As an advocate for continuous improvement, I find Kaizen principles to be an excellent fit for world-class business execution.

By adopting these principles, organisations can achieve several benefits. Firstly, identifying and eliminating inefficiencies in processes can lead to improved process effectiveness, better cost management and increased productivity over time.

Secondly, Kaizen encourages involving all team members in identifying and implementing process enhancements, creating a culture of continuous improvement.

Third, streamlining processes and reducing lead times ultimately results in better customer service, leading to higher customer retention and satisfaction.

Fourth, when employees actively participate in problem-solving and process improvement, they feel empowered and engaged, leading to a motivated workforce.

Finally, Kaizen emphasises quality at every step, leading to a focus on this attribute.

However, it's important to remember that introducing any new approach can invite resistance, and sustaining momentum for ongoing improvements can be challenging. Some organisations expect immediate results when implementing Kaizen, but it must be remembered that the philosophy emphasises gradual, incremental changes. Focusing solely on outcomes may cause organisations to miss out on improved work procedures and optimised processes.

Addressing these challenges requires commitment, adaptability and a genuine desire to create a culture of continuous enhancement. Once you start the journey and see the results, you'll never look back. So, for what it's worth, my take is that Kaizen principles promote a dynamic and adaptable business environment, leading to sustainable growth and success if handled properly.

The art of selling

As professionals, we all know that selling is an essential skill that everyone should possess. Whether you're an executive, a salesperson or a marketer, it's crucial to learn how to sell, handle objections and close deals. I recently had a conversation with some salespeople about the best sales quotes they had heard, and we all agreed that everyone in an organisation should take a selling course or spend time selling to customers. It's the best training for dealing with peers and colleagues internally, and it helps us understand the hard work that goes into closing a deal, no matter how big or small.

Here are the top 10 most valuable sales quotes:

1. People buy people – then they buy product.
2. Sell the transformation, not the product.
3. People don't care about your offer, only what your offer can do for them.
4. Compete on value, not price.
5. Sales is about listening; marketing is about empathy.
6. Quantify the time limit of your offer.
7. Tell prospects your price and then shut up.
8. The market is never saturated, your offer just sucked.
9. There is no such thing as a high price, only little value.
10. A happy customer is the most powerful form of advertising.

Remember, people buy with emotion and then justify their decisions with logic. It's important to be honest with your prospects and not sacrifice your reputation for money. And finally, be clear about what you're representing. If what you're selling is confusing, nobody will buy it.

Value disciplines

Lately, I've been thinking about the importance of values for organisations. Value disciplines are essential for any organisation to excel in what they do. It's not just about price; it's also about the effort someone must make to purchase a product or service.

To take up a good value position, an organisation must observe the four rules of procedure.

1. Try to be the best by excelling in one of the value disciplines.
2. Maintain threshold standards on value disciplines.
3. Control the market by improving value year after year.

4. Support the value discipline you have opted for by delivering a well-chosen (operating) organisational model.

   There are three value disciplines an organisation can opt for:
   1. operational excellence;
   2. customer intimacy; and
   3. product leadership.

Operational excellence focuses on cost leadership and aims to provide customers with high-quality products or services at competitive prices. Customer intimacy works on the belief that customers are the most important aspect of any organisation and delivers a mainly tailor-made approach and one-on-one solutions. Product leadership focuses on product development and innovation and the desire to be the market leader of the specific product and/or service.

Does your organisation think like this? If not, it's time to assess its strengths, market position, customer needs and organisational culture to select the discipline that aligns best with its capabilities and market strategy.

Strive for 5

Strategic planning is crucial for any business to succeed. But where do you start? The 'Strive for 5' approach breaks it down into five essential and steps.

1. **Gather the team.** First, assemble a small, dedicated team of key strategic planners to guide the development and execution of the plan. This team will gather crucial information, including relevant industry and market data, customer insights, employee feedback, a balanced scorecard and a SWOT analysis.

2. **Classify your goals.** Classify your company's goals and objectives. Define your purpose by drawing inspiration from your vision, mission and current position.

3. **Metrics that matter.** Develop your strategic plan and determine metrics such as yearly objectives, related key results and KPIs, and a high-level project roadmap. The metrics that matter.

4. **Re-communicate.** Communicate your plan clearly to your entire organisation and integrate it into daily operations.

5. **Review results.** Finally, regularly review and manage your plan to ensure it is aligned with your organisation's vision and goals.

Remember, strategic planning is an ongoing process. Follow these five steps to set your business up for success.

Eight steps for setting up benchmarking

Getting a grip on benchmarking can help your business gain a better understanding of the competition, improve performance and evaluate performance based on existing data. Recently, I shared the importance of benchmarking as an objective way to measure performance against the competition. To help the participants understand the concept, I asked them to close their eyes and imagine an octopus with its tentacles stretching out to help grow their business.

Here are my basic eight steps for setting up benchmarking:

1. Identify and understand the data, processes and functions that need to be benchmarked.

2. Organise an internal team for the design and implementation of the benchmarking tool and process.

3. Understand the process and related activities, ensuring equivalence to find relevant benchmarks for improving performance across the business.

4. Research and gather performance data.

5. Analyse the data and identify performance gaps between your entities and 'best in class' benchmarks.

6. Finalise the benchmark standards and assess their impacts.
7. Pick no more than seven metrics to benchmark, choosing carefully as these become the gold standard to work towards.
8. Apply the benchmarks and continuously update the data, making it part of your continuous business cycle and communication loop associated with your strategic plan.

Remember, customer service benchmarks are the best types of benchmarks, and it's critical to have a solid understanding of the function or process to find the right one. Finding financial-related benchmark data is not too difficult, as they are part of your current financial reports. Always remember to benchmark against the best. You are not interested in average performance.

The 9 vital vanilla strategies
As old as the Parthenon itself, there are nine 'vanilla' strategies that have always been relied upon to support strategic business planning. These include defending the core, optimising the business and driving sales capability. However, it's worth noting that even when adhering to these strategies, many large companies still fall over. Why is this?

There are some risks to consider that shouldn't be ignored. Vanilla strategies often involve playing it safe and sticking to conventional approaches, which can lead to a lack of differentiation in the market. Without a unique selling proposition (USP), your business risks becoming irrelevant. Additionally, following these strategies might lead to complacency within the organisation, hindering growth and responsiveness to changing market dynamics.

Vanilla strategies may also overlook emerging trends, disruptive technologies or untapped markets. By sticking to the tried-and-tested, you might miss out on lucrative opportunities. Relying heavily on existing clients or a single product line can be risky, and external factors such as recessions, regulatory changes or industry disruptions can impact your business.

Remember that every business context is unique, and what works for one company may not work for another. It's essential to assess risks carefully, adapt when necessary and strike a balance between stability and agility.

Procrastination and the PNR strategy

An essential aspect of strategic execution is the ability to manage procrastination. It's the biggest strategy killer for top businesses and executives. Yet it often creeps in, affecting decision making and resulting in paralysis. Whether it's the fear of making a monumental mistake or too many opinions clouding the decision space, procrastination can be a company killer.

So, what's the solution? A PNR – **P**oint of **N**o **R**eturn – strategy could be the answer. In the times of historical leaders such as Alexander the Great and Cortes, the only choices were to perish or succeed. While we may not command armies, here are three modern-day steps to tackle procrastination.

1. Commit your task or issue to paper. Be specific in your approach to change.
2. Find someone to keep you accountable. A partner or mentor can remind you of your mission.
3. Decide on your punishment for failing to reach your goal. Change needs to be dynamic and transformational. Be disciplined.

These steps will help build resilience for future missions you'll undertake as an executive, leader, parent or individual. Don't just go through the motions, apply a deep sense of focus and accountability to reach the finish line. Remember, this is a commitment strategy, not a withdrawal plan.

Mintzberg's '5 Ps of Strategy'

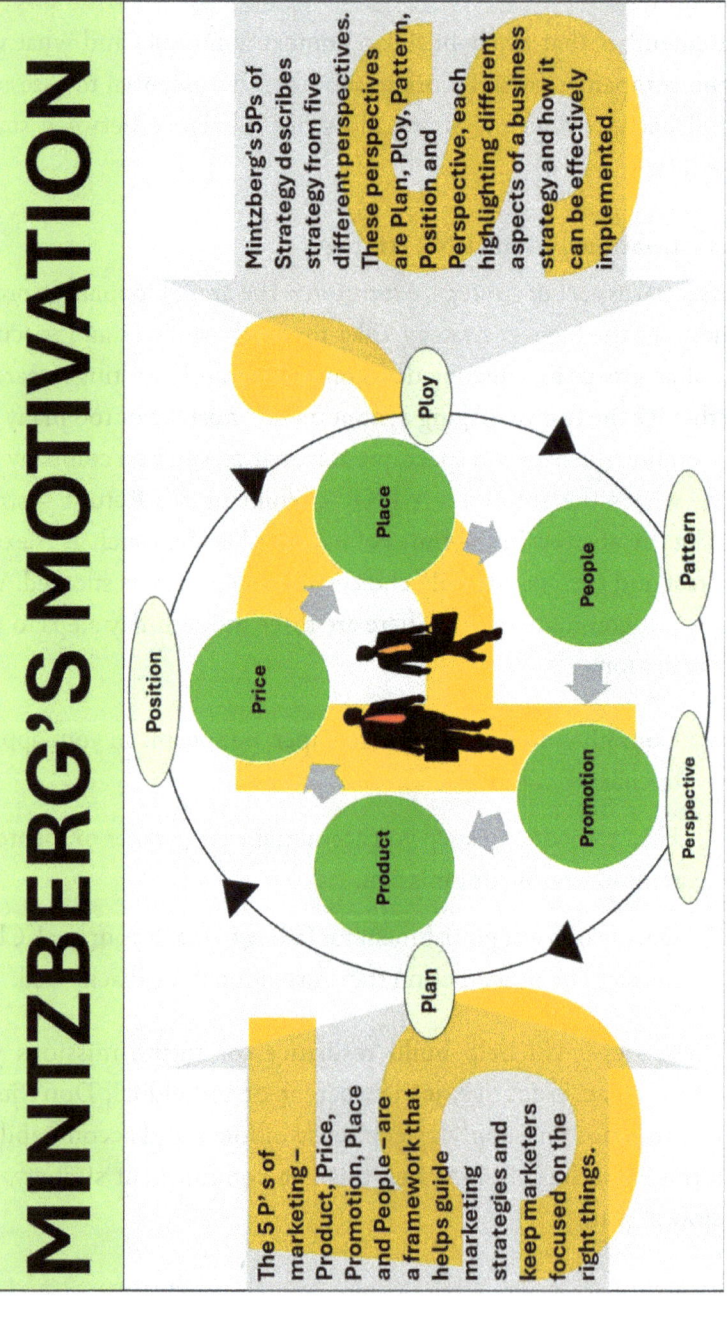

Mintzberg's '5 Ps of Strategy' plays a crucial role in business strategy for several reasons. Firstly, Mintzberg's framework goes beyond mere planning and considers various dimensions of strategy. It emphasises that strategy is not just about plans, but also about patterns, positions and perspectives.

Secondly, recognising consistent patterns in an organisation's actions helps leaders learn from the past. By understanding what has worked well (or not), they can make informed decisions.

Thirdly, the 'ploy' component acknowledges that strategy involves outsmarting competitors. Businesses need to be agile and adaptive to stay ahead.

Fourthly, the concept of 'Position' highlights the importance of finding a unique spot in the market. Businesses must differentiate themselves to create value for customers.

Lastly, the 'Perspective' aspect emphasises adopting a distinct viewpoint. A strategic mindset influences decision making and shapes the organisation's direction.

In summary, Mintzberg's 5 Ps provide a comprehensive understanding of strategy, enabling businesses to navigate complexity, learn from experience and position themselves effectively.

The Diamond Model

Diamonds are Forever is one of my favourite Bond movies and it always makes me think of a strategic model I favour called the 'Diamond Model'.

Integrating the Diamond Model and the PESTLE Analysis in your strategic planning process can provide a comprehensive approach. Let's explore how you can effectively combine these two frameworks:

1. **Start with contextual understanding:** Begin by conducting a thorough PESTLE analysis. Understand the external environment, including political, economic, social, technological, legal and environmental factors. Identify trends, risks and opportunities that impact your business.

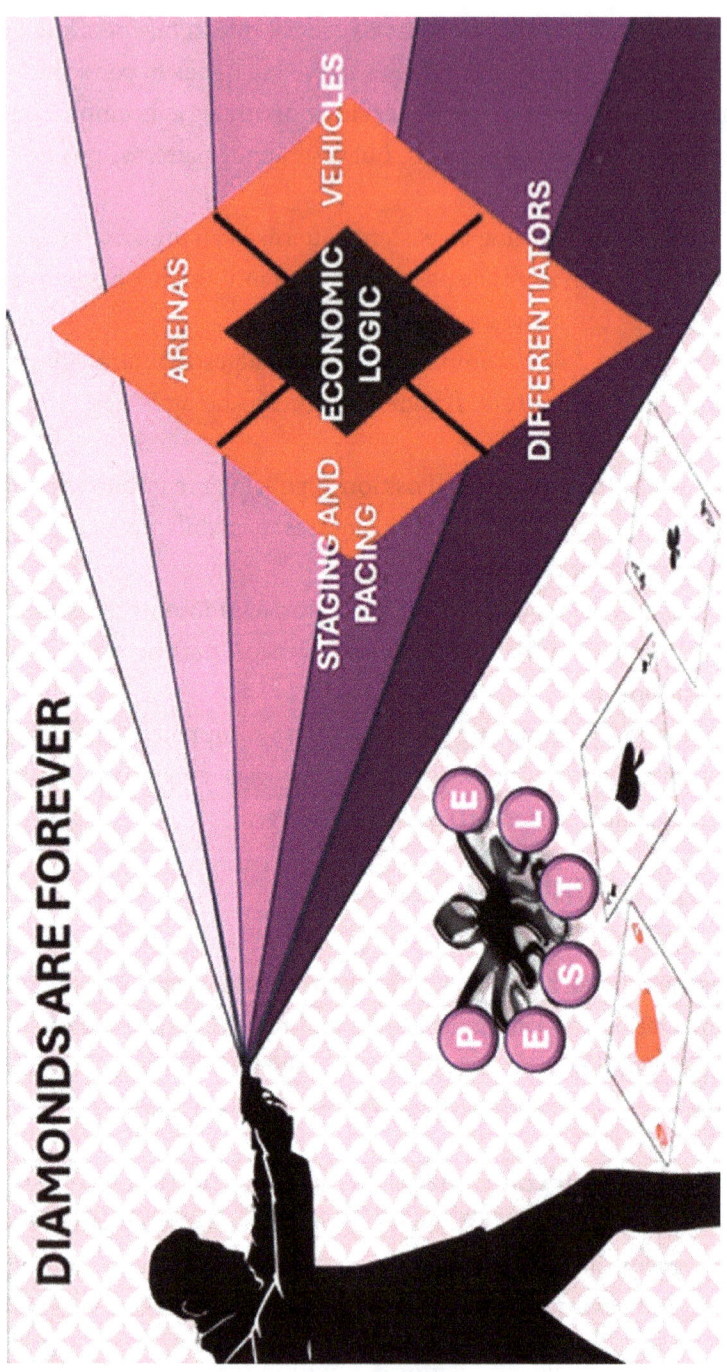

2. **Align arenas and external factors:** Map the PESTLE factors to the arenas defined in the Diamond Model. Consider how each external factor influences your business's strategic choices – for example:

    P. **Political factors:** How do government policies affect your chosen market segments or geographic regions?

    E. **Economic factors:** How does the economic climate impact your differentiation strategies?

    S. **Social factors:** How do societal trends align with your unique selling points?

    T. **Technological factors.** How can technological advancements enhance your 'vehicles', or delivery channels?

    L. **Legal factors:** How do legal frameworks shape your staging decisions?

    E. **Environmental factors:** How can environmental considerations be integrated into your economic logic?

3. **Evaluate differentiators and adaptability:** Use Mintzberg's perspective and prepare elements to assess how your differentiators align with external trends. Consider how your organisation's culture and shared beliefs influence strategic decisions. Ensure your strategy remains adaptable to changing external conditions.

4. **Strategic decision making:** Leverage the Diamond Model's vehicles and staging elements to make informed decisions. Based on the PESTLE insights, choose appropriate channels, partnerships and timing for strategic moves. Consider both short-term and long-term implications.

5. **Monitor and adjust:** Continuously monitor external factors using the PESTLE lens. Regularly revisit your strategic choices based on changing contexts. Be prepared to adjust your strategy as needed.

6. **Communication and alignment:** Clearly communicate the integrated strategy to stakeholders. Ensure alignment across different dimensions (arenas, differentiators, economic logic, vehicles and staging).

Remember that these frameworks are complementary. The Diamond Model provides a holistic view of strategy, while the PESTLE Analysis focuses on external factors. By integrating them, you create a robust and adaptable strategic planning process that considers both internal and external dynamics.

Case Study: The McDonald's model

Recently, I was having a burger with a recruiter, and we were talking about McDonald's. He asked me, of all the various strategic models I had written about on LinkedIn so far, which would most suitably be applied to McDonald's. I replied that I believed McDonald's' strategic plan revolved around three core pillars:

1. **Retain:** Strengthening and expanding areas of strength, such as breakfast.
2. **Regain:** Focusing on convenience and value to win back lost customers.
3. **Convert:** Emphasising coffee and other offerings to attract casual customers.

These three pillars have guided McDonald's through three initiatives of driving growth and maximising benefits for customers in the shortest time possible. If you applied the PESTLE Analysis, Mintzberg's 5 Ps of Strategy and the Diamond Model to McDonald's, this is how they would look.

1. **PESTLE Analysis Integration**
   - **Political:** McDonald's considers government policies related to food safety, labour laws and taxation in various countries.

- **Economic:** Economic conditions impact McDonald's' pricing strategy, cost management and global expansion decisions.
- **Social:** Demographic trends (such as health consciousness) influence menu offerings and marketing campaigns.
- **Technological:** McDonald's adapts to digital ordering, automation and delivery technologies.
- **Legal:** Compliance with food safety regulations and intellectual property laws.
- **Environmental:** Sustainability initiatives, waste reduction and energy efficiency.

2. **Mintzberg's 5 Ps Integration**
   - **Plan:** McDonald's develops a detailed strategic plan for the next five years, focusing on menu innovation, digital transformation and sustainability.
   - **Ploy:** McDonald's strategically competes by emphasising breakfast offerings, food quality and convenience.
   - **Pattern:** Over time, McDonald's consistently invests in R&D, maintains a global presence and adapts to changing consumer preferences.
   - **Position:** McDonald's' competitive position is based on its global reach, brand recognition and efficient supply chain.
   - **Perspective:** McDonald's' organisational culture emphasises customer-centricity, operational excellence and community engagement.

3. **Diamond Model integration**
   - **Arenas:** McDonald's competes in various markets (fast food, breakfast, coffee, etc.) across different regions.
   - **Differentiators:** Unique features include the iconic Big Mac, Happy Meals and the McCafé brand.

- **Vehicles:** McDonald's uses franchising, drive-thrus and mobile apps for delivery.
- **Staging:** Strategic moves are timed for maximum impact (e.g., launching new menu items during peak seasons).
- **Economic logic:** Profitability is driven by cost-effective operations and high sales volumes. McDonald's' use of a holistic approach to strategy that integrates insights, guides planning and ensures cultural alignment, is probably one of the biggest reasons they are still going strong, despite recent challenges.

Useful micro strategies to try

When building teams and working on delivering the vision and mission of your team through shared values, goals and aspirations, there are times team members may feel overwhelmed by the mere thought of executing a large-scale project through the lens of a singular strategic approach. That is why it's important that you know the people in your team well enough to give them ownership and autonomy of some unconventional approaches, or micro strategies as I call them.

There are many unconventional strategies that can lead to breakthroughs and unique outcomes if a team finds itself at an impasse on a particular aspect of your plan. Here are some unconventional approaches in both business and life that team members can reference and apply to help deliver better outcomes:

1. **Blue ocean strategy:** Rather than competing head-to-head in existing markets (red oceans), create new market spaces (blue oceans) where competition is irrelevant. Focus on innovation and value creation.
2. **Inversion thinking:** Instead of asking how to achieve success, consider what would lead to failure. Identify potential pitfalls and work backward to avoid them.

3. **Lateral thinking:** Challenge conventional thought patterns. Look for creative solutions by approaching problems from unexpected angles. Edward de Bono popularised this concept.
4. **The wishbone strategy:** Break the wishbone like a biomechanical engineer: choke up, stay firm and win the lucky side!
5. **The paradox of choice:** In business, offering too many choices can overwhelm customers. Sometimes, simplifying options leads to better decision making.
6. **The 80/20 rule (Pareto principle):** Focus on the 20% of efforts that yield 80% of results. Prioritise tasks and resources accordingly.
7. **The oblique strategies**: Created by musician Brian Eno, these cards provide random, cryptic prompts to break creative blocks. Try one when stuck!
8. **The power of constraints**: Limitations can spark creativity. Set constraints (e.g., time, budget) to force innovative thinking.
9. **The pre-mortem technique:** Imagine your project has failed. Identify the reasons why. Then address those risks proactively.
10. **The 'no' strategy:** Say 'no' more often. Focus on essential tasks and avoid distractions.

Remember, unconventional strategies challenge the status quo and encourage fresh perspectives. Team members will feel exhilarated that they can have avenues to express themselves in a creative and positive way. Try exploring and adapting these approaches to your context next time you get stuck.

Seven micro strategies for defending the core

Defending your core products is crucial for long-term business success, but how do you do it in today's ever-changing retail landscape? Here are some micro-strategic approaches to defend your core against modern-day issues:

1. **Understand consumer behaviour:** With the acceleration of online shopping and the escalating cost of living, it's crucial to anticipate and adapt to these shifts. Optimise your offerings based on consumer preferences.
2. **Embrace digital transformation:** Invest in robust e-commerce capabilities and integrate online and offline channels. Offer click-and-collect, kerbside pickup and personalised recommendations.
3. **Optimise supply chains:** Enhance supply chain agility and build resilient supply networks. Diversify suppliers and explore local sourcing.
4. **Prioritise talent development:** Identify gaps in your workforce and invest in training and development. Attract skilled professionals who understand retail dynamics.
5. **Stay customer-centric:** Continuously gather data on customer preferences and use analytics to tailor offerings. Offer personalised recommendations and loyalty programs.
6. **Innovate responsibly:** Align with sustainability trends and be transparent about sourcing, production and labour practices.
7. **Collaborate with partners:** Strengthen ties with suppliers and join industry associations to share best practices.

Remember, defending core products requires agility, customer focus and strategic foresight. Adapt to the evolving retail landscape and position your brand for success.

Bowman's strategy

A friend and I were recently discussing pricing elements in business. We agreed that in today's marketplace, most goods and services can be

Peter Sinodinos   161

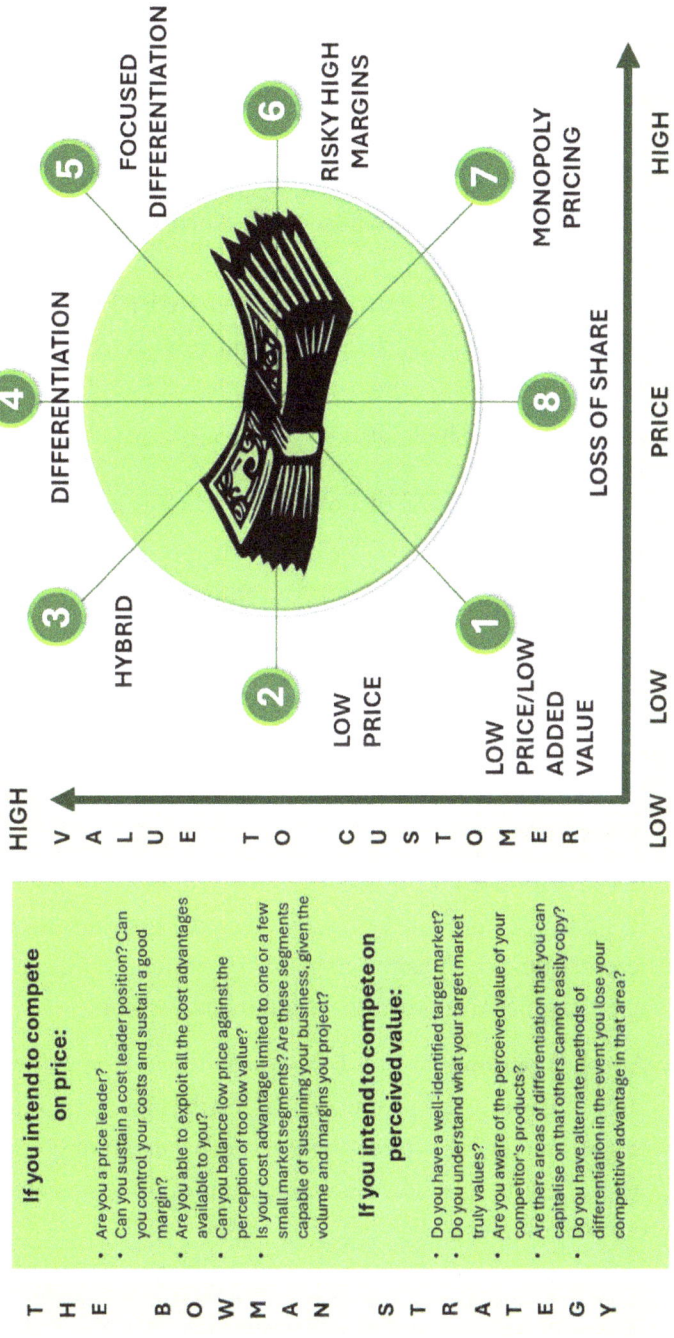

THE BOW MAN

If you intend to compete on price:

- Are you a price leader?
- Can you sustain a cost leader position? Can you control your costs and sustain a good margin?
- Are you able to exploit all the cost advantages available to you?
- Can you balance low price against the perception of too low value?
- Is your cost advantage limited to one or a few small market segments? Are these segments capable of sustaining your business, given the volume and margins you project?

STRATEGY

If you intend to compete on perceived value:

- Do you have a well-identified target market?
- Do you understand what your target market truly values?
- Are you aware of the perceived value of your competitor's products?
- Are there areas of differentiation that you can capitalise on that others cannot easily copy?
- Do you have alternate methods of differentiation in the event you lose your competitive advantage in that area?

purchased from any number of companies. This means that customers have a tremendous amount of choice, making pricing strategy the main differentiator for success. This means it's the job of companies to find their competitive edge and meet customers' needs better than the next company. My friend explained the principles behind 'Bowman's Strategy' to me. He had been exposed to it when he did his MBA many years ago.

Bowman's Strategy is a framework developed by economists Cliff Bowman and David Faulkner. Its primary purpose is to help companies understand their position in the market relative to their rivals, thus gaining a competitive edge. Here's how it works:

1. **The two dimensions of Bowman's Strategy are:**
   - price, which refers to the cost of the product or service; and
   - perceived value, which represents how customers view the value of the product, service or brand.

2. **There are eight strategic positions to consider:** These eight possible strategies are divided into four quadrants based on the combination of price and perceived value. These are shown in the diagram above.

   For example, A = Low price and low added value. Companies in this position compete primarily on price. Their products lack differentiation, and customers perceive minimal value. It's not the most competitive position within the framework.

   Another example is B = Low price. These companies produce large quantities of products. Their offerings are valued in the target market, and price wars often occur among competitive brands. Although individual product profit margins are low, high output volumes compensate.

   The remaining six positions follow similar principles, varying in price and perceived value.

3. **Making strategic decisions easier:** Companies can choose their position on the Bowman's Strategy wheel based on competitive advantage. Understanding these fundamental strategic positions enables better analysis and evaluation of the current strategy the business has in place around products. Necessary adjustments can then be made to improve competitive positioning and customer perception based on the market analysis and competitor activity, both online and offline.

In summary, Bowman's Strategy assists organisations in assessing their competitive landscape and identifying potential strategic options. By mastering these, companies can enhance their market positions and achieve their business objectives. It's a great way to test how you and your team think about your products and services. Lastly, combined with a portfolio strategy, this process at least creates awareness, if not a powerful reflection tool, for success in the future.

Blue Ocean strategy
In my review of all the great business strategies out there – and there are many – Blue Ocean Strategy is one of the most powerful. It's a business framework that aims to create new and uncontested market spaces, often referred to as 'Oceans'. Let's swim out past the breakers and dive into the key aspects of it.

Blue Ocean Strategy involves the simultaneous pursuit of differentiation and low cost to open fresh market space and generate new demand in your competitive space. It challenges the conventional belief that market boundaries and industry structures are fixed. Instead, it asserts that these boundaries can be reconstructed through the actions and beliefs of industry players.

What makes this interesting is that there are existing Red Oceans, which represent existing industries. These are defined as the known market space. In Red Oceans, companies compete within well-defined industry boundaries, striving to outperform rivals and capture a larger share of existing demand. However, as markets become crowded, profits shrink due to intense competition.

Blue Oceans denote unexplored market space – untainted by competition. Here, companies create and capture new demand rather than fighting over existing demand. The rules of the game are yet to be set, making competition irrelevant and exciting for new ventures. The number one question anyone will ask is: What are the salient differences between Red Oceans and Blue Oceans?

- **Red Ocean Strategy:** Competes in the existing market space, focuses on beating competitors exploits existing demand, balances the trade-off between value and cost, and aligns activities with either differentiation or low cost.
- **Blue Ocean Strategy:** Creates uncontested market space, makes competition irrelevant, generates and captures new demand, breaks the value-cost trade-off and aligns all activities toward differentiation and low cost.

To understand why Blue Ocean is an interesting concept, have a look at these examples:

- **Cirque du Soleil:** Instead of competing head-to-head with traditional circuses, Cirque du Soleil redefined the entertainment industry by combining elements of theatre, circus and artistry.
- **Southwest Airlines, USA:** Southwest created a Blue Ocean by offering low-cost, no-frills air travel, appealing to a broader customer base.
- **Yellow Tail Wines:** Yellow Tail disrupted the wine industry by introducing approachable, affordable wines that resonated with consumers.

Remember, Blue Ocean strategy encourages value innovation – identifying new customer needs and preferences and offering unique products or services to meet them. By doing so, companies can chart their course towards profitable growth in uncharted waters.

The 5Ps: a tried and tested comprehensive marketing framework

The 5Ps of marketing – Product, Price, Place, Promotion and People – form a comprehensive framework that guides marketers in creating effective strategies to meet consumer needs and achieve business objectives. This model, also known as the 'marketing mix', ensures that all critical aspects of marketing are considered and integrated, providing a balanced approach to market planning and execution. By focusing on these five key elements, businesses can enhance their market presence, drive sales and build lasting customer relationships.

Product

This refers to the goods or services offered by a business. It encompasses everything from design and features to quality and branding. A well-defined product strategy ensures that the offerings meet the needs and preferences of the target market. This involves continuous product development, innovation and refinement to stay competitive. Marketers must also consider the product's lifecycle and adapt strategies for introduction, growth, maturity and decline stages. A strong product strategy ensures that the business delivers value to customers and stands out in the marketplace.

Price

Price represents the amount consumers are willing to pay for a product or service. Pricing strategies are crucial as they directly impact profitability and market positioning. Businesses must consider factors such as cost of production, competition, perceived value and market demand when setting prices. Various pricing strategies, including penetration pricing, skimming and competitive pricing, can be employed based on the market context and business objectives. An effective pricing strategy balances affordability for customers and profitability for the business, contributing to sustainable growth.

Place

Place involves the distribution channels through which products or services reach customers, including physical locations like stores and digital platforms such as e-commerce websites. Effective distribution ensures product availability where and when customers need it, enhancing convenience and satisfaction.

Promotion

Promotion encompasses all the activities aimed at communicating the product's value proposition to the target audience, including advertising, sales promotions, public relations and digital marketing. An integrated promotion strategy ensures consistent messaging and maximises reach and engagement.

People

People refers to both the customers and the employees who interact with them. In the modern marketing landscape, the importance of customer service and employee engagement cannot be overstated.

These 5Ps provide a robust framework for developing comprehensive marketing strategies. By carefully considering and integrating these elements, businesses can effectively meet market demands, differentiate themselves from competitors and achieve long-term success.

The Retail Pentagon

With the future of retail constantly evolving, and new trends emerging every year, these same five 'Ps' – Product, Price, Promotion, Place and People – can also be applied to the methodology known as the Retail Pentagon, a concept that, surprisingly, not everyone is familiar with.

The Retail Pentagon is a tool that was created many years ago by two McKinsey professors to help retailers build a competitive advantage by focusing on these five key dimensions of their business. While each dimension can be as detailed as the next, it's important to note that, in general, a retailer can only truly be an authority on two at most.

Product

It almost goes without saying that without a great *Product*, your business will not succeed. Obvious and important things to consider about your product include quality, appearance, packaging, functionality and warranty.

Price

As an example, focusing on supermarkets and groceries, Aldi would appear to be the authority on *Price* – especially considering the recent major investigation into price gouging and cost-of-living pressures. Aldi is usually anywhere between 7–16% cheaper for groceries based on my personal wallet experience.

Promotion

Promotion is often the most hotly contested topic in any organisation, especially when performance is below expectations across the business. It is one of the basic elements of the market mix and one of the most important in the Retail Pentagon – and it's often the one everyone believes they are an expert in.

The aim of promotion is to increase brand awareness, create interest, generate sales and create brand loyalty. However, effective marketing needs to be a sustained focus to inform target audiences of the relative merits of a product, service or brand persuasively. It must help marketers to create a distinctive place in customers' minds and can be done in either a cognitive or emotional way.

With social media and the likes of Google Analytics to track performance – not to mention so many other online platforms to tell a story – marketing requires real skill to be able to manage all these streams successfully and tell a significant and consistent story to consumers about the brand.

Place

The *Place* factor of the pentagon is where the product/service of the business is seen, made, sold or distributed, as mentioned in the 5 Ps of marketing section. It's important to consider how accessible your product or service is and ensure that customers can easily find you. The product or service must be available to customers at the right time, at the right place and in the right quantity.

For example, a business may want to provide their products via an e-commerce site, at a retail store or through a third-party distributor – an omnichannel approach, which broadens impact. This means Place takes on more micro detail – visual merchandising elements and some elements of the business's nomenclature (signage) start to blur the lines with the promotion dimension, as they denote the location of the business to passers-by.

People

As has already been mentioned many times, *People* are one of the most important factors in any organisation – not just any people, but the right people. Good people who are committed to the cause, are aware of their strengths and weaknesses, and who can communicate ideas and concepts with anyone they meet, as well as manage their time well, are gold in any business.

Strategy and culture: partners in business performance

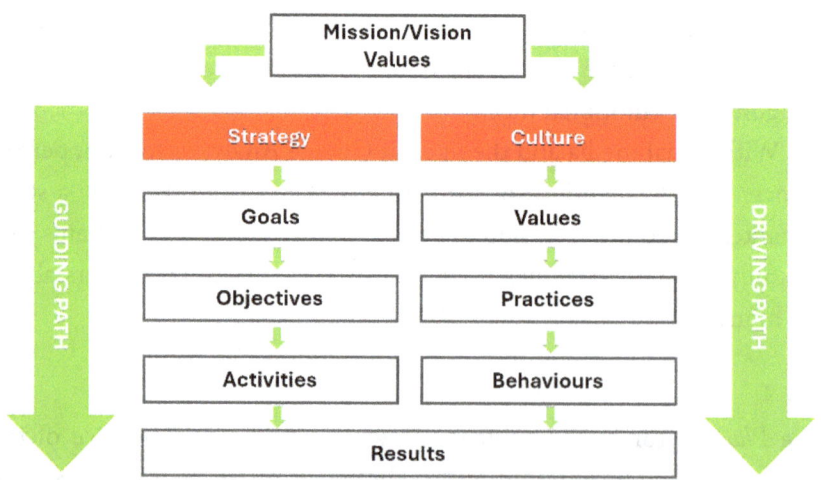

Driving strategy and social momentum are essential in creating a strong company culture, according to a recent conversation I had with a happy business owner. This dynamic feedback loop between culture and strategy ensures that an organisation's identity remains aligned with its objectives.

Effective communication and building strong relationships across your business network are key to creating a continuous communication loop, with the final person always in mind – the customer, both internal and external.

The value of a Venn diagram

A Venn diagram can be a powerful tool for businesses to understand the relationships between different sets of information and how they intersect, with aspects such as superb leadership, flawless execution and innovation each having their own unique value in defining a successful business. When these sets intersect, they share commonalities and produce shared results.

Combining *great leadership* and *flawless execution* can result in growth, while *good leadership* and *innovation* can future-proof your business. When *execution* and *innovation* are combined, this gives you an edge in the marketplace. When they *all* intersect, they produce a unique selling proposition – in this case, a sensational retail or franchise organisation. Understanding these relationships can help you thrive and creating a Venn diagram to analyse your business's success factors will give you a clearer picture of how to achieve this.

Porter's Five Forces

Are you looking to up your strategic game? Then it's time to brush up on some key frameworks that will help you better understand and deliver with your teams.

First up is the *Ansoff Matrix*, which can help you evaluate growth initiatives and conceptualise risk associated with different product strategies. Then there's the *SWOT analysis*, a popular method of looking at an organisation's strengths, weaknesses, opportunities and threats. Another methodology, which I've already discussed, is PESTLE, which helps you delve deeper into political, economic, social, technological, legal and environmental influences on the market.

But another useful tool to consider is Michael Porter's Five Forces model, which draws from economics to determine the competitive intensity and profitability of an industry. This framework includes substitutes, rivals, new entrants, suppliers and customers. Plus, it's important to consider the power of complementary goods and service providers.

Another of Michael Porter's methodologies is the Four Corners model, a useful technique to evaluate competitors, generate insights concerning likely competitor strategy changes and determine competitor reaction to environmental changes and industry shifts. By examining a competitor's current strategy, future goals, assumptions about the market and core capabilities, the Four Corners Model helps analysts address these four core issues. Used along with the Five Forces economic model, in conjunction with a more traditional static model such as SWOT, Porter's Four Corners is a great way to consider competitive behaviours against a backdrop of analytical and assumptive processes.

All of these frameworks are critical to your strategic thinking. As Porter himself said, "If all you're trying to do is essentially the same thing as your rivals, then it's unlikely that you'll be very successful."

So, take some time to master these frameworks and elevate your strategic game.

CONCLUSION

I hope you have found this collection of my blogs and views on the LIPS framework (Leadership, Ideas, People and Strategy) positive. I thought a lot about LIPS as an acronym after I watched an old newsreel from the 1940s and the phrase 'Loose lips sink ships' came up.

The phrase originated during World War II as part of a broader campaign by the US Office of War Information to prevent sensitive information from being inadvertently disclosed. It was prominently featured on posters and other wartime propaganda materials, designed to remind military personnel and civilians alike of the dangers of careless talk. The underlying message was that seemingly innocent conversations could be overheard by enemy spies and potentially lead to devastating consequences, such as the sinking of ships and subsequent loss of lives.

This slogan effectively conveyed the critical importance of maintaining operational security and vigilance. By promoting the idea that even minor slips of information could have catastrophic outcomes, the campaign aimed to instil a sense of responsibility and caution in the public. The saying quickly entered the popular lexicon and has since been used more broadly to emphasise the importance of discretion and the potential risks associated with sharing confidential or sensitive information.

In my case, it's not so much about sensitive information – more about being diligent and focused on those four essential elements, i.e., Leadership, Ideas, People and Strategy, that are integral to building and sustaining a world-class business. These components work in synergy, creating a robust foundation for success in the competitive global market.

Effective **Leadership** is the cornerstone that guides the vision and direction of the organisation. Leaders inspire and motivate employees, fostering a culture of excellence and innovation. By setting clear goals and expectations, leaders ensure that every team member understands their role in achieving the company's objectives.

Ideas are the lifeblood of innovation and growth within a world-class business. An environment that encourages creative thinking and the free exchange of ideas leads to continuous improvement and adaptation. Leaders play a crucial role in cultivating this environment, providing the necessary resources and support for ideation. By valuing and implementing employees' ideas, businesses can develop unique products, services and processes that set them apart from their competitors. This constant flow of fresh perspectives drives the organisation forward and keeps it at the cutting edge of its industry.

People are at the heart of any world-class business. A talented, motivated and well-trained workforce is crucial for executing the company's strategy and bringing innovative ideas to life. Investing in employee development, engagement and well-being ensures that the organisation attracts and retains top talent. Leaders must create a supportive and inclusive culture where employees feel valued and empowered to contribute their best work. By recognising and leveraging the diverse skills and perspectives of their people, businesses can enhance their performance and achieve sustained success.

Finally, a well-formulated **Strategy** is essential for aligning the organisation's resources and efforts with its long-term goals. Strategic planning involves setting clear objectives, identifying key initiatives and allocating resources effectively. It provides a roadmap for translating innovative ideas into actionable plans. Leaders must ensure that the strategy is communicated clearly throughout the organisation and that all employees are engaged in its execution. By doing so, the strategy becomes a unifying force that aligns all departments and teams towards common goals, fostering a cohesive and focused effort.

In conclusion, the harmony of Leadership, Ideas, People and Strategy is what enables a business to succeed. Each element reinforces and supports the others, creating a dynamic and resilient organisation capable of thriving in a complex and ever-changing environment. Effective leadership sets the direction, innovative ideas drive growth, strategic planning ensures alignment and a dedicated workforce executes the vision. Together, these elements form a powerful framework that propels the organisation towards excellence and long-term success.

Thank you for taking the time to read *LIPS*. I truly hope that you've found insights within these pages that resonate with your experiences and inspire new approaches on your journey. This book was crafted with the belief that leadership, creativity, people, and strategy are all essential elements that shape not only our professional achievements but also our personal growth. I hope you leave with practical takeaways and reflective ideas that can support you as you face challenges and strive for your own goals.

As you've seen throughout LIPS, the journey is ongoing. Leadership, Ideas, People, and Strategy are not static, they're dynamic elements that require constant adaptation. In a world that's always evolving, so must we. Applying these four pillars is a continuous work in progress, one that demands awareness, flexibility, and resilience as our environments and the people around us change. Thank you again for joining me on this exploration. I hope *LIPS* serves as a lasting resource that you'll return to as you refine your path forward.

BIBLIOGRAPHY

Strategy

1. "Competitive Strategy: Techniques for Analysing Industries and Competitors" by Michael E. Porter
2. "Blue Ocean Strategy: How to Create Uncontested Market Space and Make the Competition Irrelevant" by W. Chan Kim and Renée Mauborgne
3. "Good Strategy Bad Strategy: The Difference and Why It Matters" by Richard P. Rumelt
4. "The Art of Strategy: A Game Theorist's Guide to Success in Business and Life" by Avinash K. Dixit and Barry J. Nalebuff
5. "Playing to Win: How Strategy Really Works" by A.G. Lafley and Roger L. Martin

Leadership

1. "Leadership: In Turbulent Times" by Doris Kearns Goodwin
2. "Leaders Eat Last: Why Some Teams Pull Together and Others Don't" by Simon Sinek
3. "The Five Dysfunctions of a Team: A Leadership Fable" by Patrick Lencioni
4. "Drive: The Surprising Truth About What Motivates Us" by Daniel H. Pink

5. "The Leadership Challenge: How to Make Extraordinary Things Happen in Organizations" by James M. Kouzes and Barry Z. Posner

Ideation

1. "Where Good Ideas Come From: The Natural History of Innovation" by Steven Johnson
2. "Creative Confidence: Unleashing the Creative Potential Within Us All" by Tom Kelley and David Kelley
3. "The Innovator's Dilemma: When New Technologies Cause Great Firms to Fail" by Clayton M. Christensen
4. "Thinkertoys: A Handbook of Creative-Thinking Techniques" by Michael Michalko
5. "The Art of Innovation: Lessons in Creativity from IDEO, America's Leading Design Firm" by Tom Kelley

People Management

1. "The Human Side of Enterprise" by Douglas McGregor
2. "First, Break All the Rules: What the World's Greatest Managers Do Differently" by Marcus Buckingham and Curt Coffman
3. "Drive: The Surprising Truth About What Motivates Us" by Daniel H. Pink
4. "The 7 Habits of Highly Effective People: Powerful Lessons in Personal Change" by Stephen R. Covey
5. "Principles: Life and Work" by Ray Dalio

Articles and Papers
Strategy
1. Porter, M. E. (1996). "What is Strategy?" Harvard Business Review.
2. Rumelt, R. P. (2011). "The Perils of Bad Strategy." McKinsey Quarterly.
3. Kim, W. C., & Mauborgne, R. (2004). "Blue Ocean Strategy." Harvard Business Review.

Leadership
1. Goleman, D. (1998). "What Makes a Leader?" Harvard Business Review.
2. Kotter, J. P. (1995). "Leading Change: Why Transformation Efforts Fail." Harvard Business Review.
3. Sinek, S. (2009). "How Great Leaders Inspire Action." TED Talk.

Ideation
1. Christensen, C. M. (1995). "Disruptive Technologies: Catching the Wave." Harvard Business Review.
2. Amabile, T. M. (1998). "How to Kill Creativity." Harvard Business Review.
3. Johnson, S. (2010). "Where Good Ideas Come From." TED Talk.

People Management
1. Herzberg, F. (1968). "One More Time: How Do You Motivate Employees?" Harvard Business Review.
2. Pfeffer, J. (1998). "The Human Equation: Building Profits by Putting People First." Harvard Business Review.
3. Pink, D. H. (2009). "The Puzzle of Motivation." TED Talk.

Other Resources
Online Courses and Lectures

1. **Harvard Business School Online** - Courses on Leadership and Management, Strategy Execution.

2. **Coursera** - Courses such as "Foundations of Business Strategy" by the University of Virginia, "Creative Problem Solving" by the University of Minnesota.

3. **LinkedIn Learning** - Various courses on Leadership, Strategy, and Innovation.

Journals and Publications

1. **Harvard Business Review**
2. **MIT Sloan Management Review**
3. **Journal of Business Strategy**
4. **Strategic Management Journal**
5. **Leadership Quarterly**

ABOUT THE AUTHOR

Peter Sinodinos is a strategist, leadership expert and advocate for people development. Based in Sydney, Australia, he specialises in conducting workshops that empower retail and franchising clients to harness the power of strategic alignment for sustainable growth and success. This is his first book.

Connect with Peter at: https://petersinodinos.com

www.ingramcontent.com/pod-product-compliance
Lightning Source LLC
Chambersburg PA
CBHW051927160426
43198CB00012B/2068